T0277671

IMAGES
of Aviation

AVIATION IN THE
ADIRONDACKS

In October 1912, a 31-year-old aviator, George Gray, became the first pilot to land in the Adirondacks, when he set his Wright-Burgess Model B biplane down on a farmer's field in Vermontville, just a few miles from the village of Saranac Lake. Gray's arrival was a sensation and remarkably well-documented. Local businessman William Kollecker (left) photographed Gray both on the ground and in the air during his activities in Saranac Lake. Today, his photographs provide excellent documentation of the first flight in the Adirondacks. (Courtesy of Saranac Lake Free Library Adirondack Research Room.)

ON THE COVER: Following the success of the Model T in the automobile industry, Henry Ford leaped into the nascent aircraft industry. The Ford Trimotor aircraft, affectionately known as the "Tin Goose," featured numerous innovations, not least of which was passenger comfort in an enclosed cabin. Only 199 of these all-metal aircraft were produced, yet some may still be seen in museums and even in flight. (Courtesy of Saranac Lake Free Library Adirondack Research Room.)

IMAGES
of Aviation

AVIATION IN THE ADIRONDACKS

Aurora Pfaff

ARCADIA
PUBLISHING

Copyright © 2024 by Aurora Pfaff
ISBN 978-1-4671-6154-1

Published by Arcadia Publishing
Charleston, South Carolina

Printed in the United States of America

Library of Congress Control Number: 2023952173

For all general information, please contact Arcadia Publishing:
Telephone 843-853-2070
Fax 843-853-0044
E-mail sales@arcadiapublishing.com

Visit us on the Internet at www.arcadiapublishing.com

For Michael Shinagel, in gratitude for your wisdom and friendship, and for my mother, Mary. Please don't cry on the pages of the book.

CONTENTS

ACKNOWLEDGMENTS

Many people contributed to this project to bring it to print, from offering cheerful support to the loan of photographs, passing along names and stories, and nudging encouragement. My husband, Bill, was unceasingly supportive, enthusiastic, and entirely willing to drive me all over the Adirondacks in search of photographs. The excitement, enthusiasm, and attitude of "it was bound to happen" from my parents was both a delight and a source of encouragement.

This, my first book, came about thanks to a lifetime of looking up and was made possible thanks to the wonderful team at Arcadia, particularly Jeff Ruetsche and the ever-diligent (and patient) Caroline Vickerson.

The images in this volume appear courtesy of a number of organizations. For the sake of brevity in the text, some of their names are abbreviated. The list of organizations is as follows— Adirondack Experience: The Museum on Blue Mountain Lake (ADKX), Saranac Lake Free Library Adirondack Research Room (SLFLARR), Historic Saranac Lake, Town of Webb Historical Association (TOWHA), Keene Valley Library (KVL), Texas Woman's University (TWU), Hamilton County Historian (HCH), Speculator Lake Pleasant Town Historical Society Inc. (SLPHS Inc.), Wilmington Historical Society (WHS), Goff-Nelson Memorial Library in Tupper Lake (GNML), the Library of Congress, Glenn H. Curtiss Museum (GHCM), Wright State University (WSU), Schlesinger Library at the Harvard Radcliffe Institute, and the US Naval History and Heritage Command (USNHHC). Also credited for their amazing contributions are Frederick and Cynthia Adcock, Jim Catalano, Town of Champion historian Lynn Thornton, Lamar Bliss, and Tim Helms. All other images without courtesy lines are from the author's personal collection or are in the public domain.

All of the people I worked with at these organizations, including Santa Claus himself (also known as Clarence Russell), were full of kindness and enthusiasm and were of immense help. They have my grateful thanks.

INTRODUCTION

In the late summer of 2022, after many years of thinking about it, I finally took my first flying lesson. It was, as I am sure many other pilots can attest, a beautiful experience, full of eye-opening sights and sensations. Flying offered the opportunity to see a place I thought I knew in a completely different way. In the air, the Adirondacks seem, paradoxically, to be both immense and small. Before long, as I learned to ease my white-knuckle grip on the yoke of a Piper Cherokee, I started to wonder about who else flies in the Adirondacks and who had flown in the past. That is the very simple story of how this book came to be.

For over 100 years, aviation has played its important part in Adirondack history, from the moments when children see their first plane to the pioneers who made the first flights, the generations of families that have made air travel a way of life in the backcountry, and more. The Adirondacks have seen airfields come and go, famous aviators—and aviatrixes—brighten the skies with stunts, and have even played a role in the war effort.

George Gray made the first flight over the Adirondacks in 1912, but his could have just as easily been the second. The second person to do something is not usually recorded, and countless aviators have flown over the Adirondacks, landed on farmer's fields, and helped cobble together new airports with nothing but a windsock, a hangar, and some gumption. It may never be possible to know all of their names but each has played his, her, or their role in the history of aviation in this extraordinary, wild, beautiful place.

Aviation has had a profound impact on life in the Adirondacks, for no sooner did the first planes arrive than aviation became not just a novelty or something fun and exciting to see, but it also changed how life was lived. Travel could now be done by plane, rather than train or road, at a time when planes might seem dangerous, but trips by car or train were long and often laborious. Thus, getting to and from the Adirondacks could now be done in a much faster manner. This ease of use extended itself to how the Adirondacks was used as a backdrop and place for wilderness adventures; with airplanes an increasing presence in the region, access to the wilderness, in particular to the backcountry, became easier and more within reach for many. Gone were the days when a trip to a remote lake required days of paddling and portages. A floatplane could carry adventurers, their gear, and even canoes to a scenic spot in just an hour or two.

This book covers the period of time from 1912 to the 1950s and a bit into the 1960s. That time period was chosen because it was, in many ways, the most active, the most demonstrative of progress, change, and activity. Barnstorming led to flying circuses which led to airmail flights which led to fish stocking and wildfire suppression. There was a time when commercial air travel blossomed; the time period in which it was in decline is not covered here—save for the note that it is returning and that, once again, it is possible to fly from Saranac Lake to New York City—for purposes of focusing on the planes that have flown and of the pilots who are legendary in their own right, whether they are world-famous or relatively unknown.

No matter what type of plane or what the nature of the flight was, the natural world of the Adirondacks is always at the heart of aviation. It is the reason why many fly and why so many flights have had a greater purpose, such as dousing wildfires or studying the impacts of pollution on our most remote waterways. The natural world of the Adirondacks is why many come to the Adirondacks to begin with. Some of the pilots and adventurers in these pages were not born in the Adirondacks, but they chose to be part of it and make their lives here and, in doing so, have contributed to the story of the Adirondacks. People come to the Adirondacks because it offers a landscape of stunning beauty that has, in many, many places, been protected from development and even the modern world. Aviation makes that world accessible to us. It is also the sheer force of the Adirondacks that has required aviators to put skis on their planes or adapt to short landings, and it is what has caused some to lose their lives. No matter the skill of the aviator, the Adirondacks can be unforgiving, and although those stories are sometimes hard to hear (or in this case, read), they are important pieces of the quilt that is aviation in the Adirondack Mountains.

Many, many people have flown here since 1912. It is not possible to name them all or feature each and every one, so any omissions are not intentional or meant as a slight.

All of these stories—of planes on skis and remote adventures—are found in the pages of this book, which is an effort to share at least a glimpse of the places and the people who have taken to the skies here since 1912, sharing who those people were, what made them interesting and unique, and what made their flights so thrilling, and even simply beautiful, to relive. It is the intention of this book to share the distinctive character of what aviation has been in the Adirondack Mountains and what it has meant to so many to be part of.

One

EARLY ADVENTURES

Unlike today's planes, the Wright-Burgess Model B flown to the Adirondacks in 1912 had no enclosed hull, and the propellers were situated behind the pilot's bare-bones seat. Local photographer William Kollecker took this photograph of George Gray's plane in action; here, it is possible to see the propellers at the rear of the wings, the wheels adjacent to the skids for landing, and Gray at the controls. (Courtesy of SLFLARR.)

Among the visitors George Gray received was local hotelier Paul Smith, who asked Gray for a flight. Gray demurred, but more successful in the attempt to fly was Edith "Jack" Sterns, a young woman on vacation near Gray's original landing site in Vermontville. Sterns's adventure was made while tethered to her seat via luggage straps, as the Model B had no cockpit and only very rudimentary seats. Sterns and Gray would go on to marry and continue to fly together for several years. She would write a memoir about their flying days entitled *Up*, after their airplane. In this real-photo postcard, Gray can be seen flying low over a beach, with his name emblazoned on the aircraft's canvas "blinkers." Gray graduated from the prestigious Wright Flying School in 1911 and was leasing the plane for $500 a month, which he paid for by barnstorming and flying exhibitions.

With the world abuzz about aeroplanes, no town in the Adirondacks was immune to the excitement. When Gray made the first landing in the Adirondacks, at Fletcher's Farm in Vermontville, local excitement began with the farmer whom Gray asked for use of his telephone and spread from there. Gray had intended to land at Saranac Lake, but weather near Whiteface Mountain intervened. Soon after his arrival, visitors began to appear, including local photographer William Kollecker and one charmingly hatted dog. Gray eventually made his way to Saranac Lake, where local entrepreneur William Cooper had arranged for Gray's plane to be on display—to paying customers—and where Gray flew for crowds of hundreds of spectators. (Both, courtesy of SLFLARR.)

George Gray's trip to Saranac Lake was coordinated by local entrepreneur William Cooper, who went by the name of "Caribou Bill." Cooper was a dog sled driver who ran a silent film studio on Lower Saranac Lake; he had a flair for showmanship and bringing Gray to Saranac Lake gave the village terrific entertainment. Flights such as Gray's were naturally dangerous and breathtaking. "Jack" Gray would later recount more than one close call, including a near-fatal incident involving the plane, a fence, and a freight train. George Gray's adventures in Saranac Lake, however, were without incident and featured a thrilling event at the local racetrack: Gray in his plane racing an automobile on the ground. Vexed by the tight turns of the track, Gray put up a good fight, but the car won. (Above, courtesy of SLFLARR; below, courtesy of WSU.)

The earliest flights in the Adirondacks were not confined to warm weather months, despite open cockpits, unpredictable weather, and bitter cold. In late 1912, Saranac Lake photographer William Kollecker photographed a biplane over Saranac Lake's Lake Flower, while also capturing another photographer in the image. Instead of wheels, the plane had skis for landing on frozen lakes, a practice common in the early years of Adirondack aviation. Some of the earliest aviation adventures took place in winter, with the owners of lakeside hotels arranging for planes on skis to give their guests short excursion flights as part of their vacation. Kollecker sold many prints at his shop in downtown Saranac Lake; images of George Gray or of an adventure such as this one may have been among them. To this day, Kollecker is the best-known of Saranac Lake's photographers. (Courtesy of ADKX.)

In the shadow of Whiteface Mountain, the fifth-highest peak in the state, the first airport in Wilmington was a strip alongside the Ausable River, on land developed by William Everest, who was the proprietor of Whiteface Mountain House, an elegant nearby hotel. In this image from 1928, a biplane filling up on leaded gasoline—the top of the fuel truck may be glimpsed to the left of the plane—drew a considerable crowd of interested visitors of all ages. The airport, which was built in 1928 with two runways, was used through the 1940s, including as a base for aerial sightseeing tours. As the size of aircraft grew and aviation needs changed, the airport was not large enough to meet demand. Most recently, the land once occupied by the airport was a campground. (Courtesy of Connor & Wolfe Family Collection, WHS.)

In 1928, local residents Hazel and Bessie Olney posed next to a de Havilland Moth operated by the Albany Air Service. Aviation was still very much in its infancy when both Olney girls were born; in this image, Hazel would have been about 20 years old, and Bessie was about 17. The airport was declared open in the summer of June 1928, with the *Adirondack Record-Elizabethtown Post* reporting that it was already a popular spot for vacationers arriving from downstate. The Albany Air Service flew passengers and mail as well as offering ground school in the state capital. The de Havilland Moth was one of the most popular and best-performing aircraft of the time. Because Albany gave frequent excursion rides at the Wilmington airport, it is possible that young Hazel and Bessie had the novel experience of seeing their hometown from the air. (Courtesy of Douglas A. Wolfe Collection, WHS.)

PISECO AIRPORT, PISECO, N.Y.   506.

Officially activated as an airport in 1945, the airfield in Piseco had been in use for some years beforehand, even before the pastureland was cleared for smoother landings. Sandwiched between mountains and Piseco Lake, the airport is known for being a beautiful, if not windy, general aviation field and the site of more than one interesting incident. In 1935, a flight from Syracuse to Boston, traveling in heavy snow, crashed just south of Piseco. Despite subzero temperatures, the four men on board were eventually rescued by local residents on snowshoes. This image, from 1930, shows two planes, the nearer of which is a biplane manufactured by the WACO Aircraft Company. It was a three-seater belonging to Sanford "Sandy" Liddle, a key figure in the creation of the airport at Piseco. Born in Schenectady, Liddle grew up adventuring on Piseco Lake. As an adult, he operated an air company in Schenectady, offered sightseeing flights in Piseco, and organized model airplane events for children. Aviator Wiley Post visited Piseco and referred to the airport as "one of the few perfect flying fields."

Anding Field At Abrams Pavilion Piseco Lake Adirondacks

To this day, Piseco is a popular spot for pilots, known for challenging winds at the airport and an annual fly-in pancake breakfast. Early in the town's history, one of the most popular destinations was known simply as Abram's, an expanse of lakefront that, by the 1920s, included a beach, carousel, very popular dance hall, and rental cabins. Early aviators, such as this one, who landed on the field adjacent to the beach and picnic area, would have found themselves just steps away from an abundance of summer adventures, although the field landing might have been an adventure in and of itself. As seaplanes became popular and suited to life in the Adirondacks, Abram's would eventually install a seaplane hangar on its beach and offer short rides in the summer. (Courtesy of Frederick and Cynthia Adcock, *Piseco Lake and Arietta*.)

In the town of Arietta, home of Piseco Lake and many other smaller lakes, scenic peaks, and quiet forest, life has long centered around Piseco, where the lake and surrounding wilderness offer activities ranging from paddling and boating to hiking and hunting. It was in Piseco that William Bradley Abrams grew up and developed the vacation destination that had been started by his family. Floyd Abrams opened Abram's Sportsman's Home in the 1800s, and in the 20th century, William Bradley Abrams added delights such as a carousel, which he purchased from Sacandaga Lake, the animals for which eventually ended up at the Shelburne Museum in Vermont. Abram's eventually offered floatplane rides to guests in the Travel Air, seen here. The Travel Air went on to have an interesting fate. (Courtesy of HCH.)

Abrams Field - Air View - Piseco

One of the many advantages of aviation, at least for local residents, was the opportunity to view familiar places in a new way. This image of the field at Abram's Sportsman's Home may not seem to show much more than a field, but to see it from a bird's-eye view would have nonetheless been a great novelty. It is not a surprise, then, that postcards featuring aerial views became popular in the early years of aviation and have remained so. In Piseco, as in many other Adirondack towns, views from the air were expansive and included everything from mountain ranges to delights such as the carousel at Abram's. (Courtesy of Frederick and Cynthia Adcock, *Piseco Lake and Arietta*.)

In the particularly pretty stretch of road between Keene and Keene Valley, where the High Peaks become closer at hand, Marcy Field is a landmark for many reasons: in the summer, a farmers market occupies one part of the field, while year-round, the trailhead just beyond the field gives access to the highest peaks in the state. Marcy Field is also a notable airfield, one that has been loved by aviators since the 1930s for its sporty turf runway and for its place in local history. In 1938, the very first airmail flight from the Adirondacks took off from Marcy Field, with local physician Alphonso Goff at the controls. Marcy Field's proximity to exceptional views makes it a special runway, and although more than one hiker on Mount Marcy, the field's namesake and highest of them all, has been vexed by aviators taking in the views overhead and rumors of mooning persist, the view from the air is awe-inspiring. (Courtesy of KVL.)

Like so many of the towns and villages that dot the Adirondack landscape, the hamlet of Old Forge, a popular destination for vacationers, families, and adventurers, has a fascinating history. From early mines run by infamous characters to the influx of city dwellers looking to explore the wilderness, Old Forge has always been a notable gateway to the Adirondacks. When the first airplane landed in the village on June 21, 1919, crowds rushed to the field where the plane sat. The flight was no mere jaunt: it was a stunt crafted by the *Utica Daily Press*. Before landing, the pilot dropped bundles of the newspaper over the town, proceeded to perform stunts along the lakeshore, and eventually came to land, to the delight of all who witnessed it. (Courtesy of TOWHA.)

The excited crowds that greeted the biplane and pilot were made of people of all ages, from awed children to adults eager to view the plane, talk to the pilot, and savor the moment aviation arrived in Old Forge. While this image barely shows the airplane itself, capturing part of the crowd is an important moment as well. This was the start of Old Forge's aviation history, which would include air taxis, airplanes used as rescue and ambulance service, sightseeing flights, and public service. In 1950, a ferocious storm that has been described as "hurricane-like" blew down a tremendous amount of forest in the area. Following the storm, airplanes were utilized to take aerial photographs in order to map the damage to the dense forests. (Courtesy of TOWHA.)

This early aerial image of Lake Placid—both the village and the lake itself—shows a much different scene than the one known today. More pastoral, the Lake Placid seen here was popular as a vacation destination (Stevens House hotel is visible on the left) but still a small town. Whiteface Mountain, still a few decades away from being a ski resort, dominates the horizon. (Courtesy of SLFLARR.)

AEROPLANE VIEW OF FORT TICONDEROGA, N.Y.

Over the years, numerous aerial images have helped share Fort Ticonderoga's remarkable history. Abandoned and severely damaged after 1781, the fort lay in ruins for many years. Many illustrated aerial postcards show a colorful fort after the early-20th-century reconstruction, which so many visitors enjoy today. This stark black-and-white photograph postcard shows the period before reconstruction returned the fort to what it once was.

Within seven years of the first successful flight of any aircraft, the first successful flight of what are now known as seaplanes or floatplanes occurred in France. Floatplanes were quickly adopted in the United States, including the Adirondacks. Intrepid pilots suddenly had a new way to access wild areas, as seen in this image of a biplane floatplane on Lake Placid.

THE AGORA, FOREST HALL AND FOREST TOWERS, LAKE PLACID CLUB, N.Y.

Founded in 1895, the Lake Placid Club was a premier hotel on Mirror Lake. Although exclusionary, the club was popular for its amenities and sporting activities. In 1929, the *New York Times* began arriving in Lake Placid by plane, the paper reporting that a plane landed next to the club and that "a few minutes later guests, not long out of bed, were reading the paper on the porches."

Two

NOTABLE NAMES AND FACES

Although it had been an airfield as early as the 1920s, Lake Placid did not have an official airport until January 1939. Later that year, Charles Lindbergh landed at Lake Placid in a Curtiss P-36 fighter on behalf of the US Army Air Corps. Lindbergh's duties included recruitment and exploring potential sites for future air bases. His flight from Long Island took one hour and fifteen minutes. (Courtesy of ADKX.)

In all of the Adirondacks, there may be no name more synonymous with aviation than that of Clarence Petty. A legend in life and beloved today, Petty was a man deeply connected to the Adirondacks. Throughout his life, Petty hiked voraciously (he was a 46er many times over), tirelessly advocated for the protection of the wilderness, worked as a state forest ranger, and was an accomplished, dedicated pilot. The mark he left on the Adirondack Park cannot be overstated, as it was thanks to Petty's surveys and research of the backcountry that led to many areas being designated wild forest and wilderness areas, while his continued presence and advocacy allowed for more protection for the natural beauty of the region. Petty first glimpsed a plane in Saranac Lake when he was just a boy, watching a floatplane land on Lake Flower. This led to decades of flight for Petty, not just in the Adirondacks, but also in the Pacific in World War II. He taught others to fly for many years, running a flying school in Potsdam, not stopping until he was 94. (Courtesy of ADKX.)

In 1928, aviatrix Elinor Smith of Long Island captured the world's attention by, at the age of 17, flying underneath the four bridges on Manhattan's East River, an escapade she undertook as a dare. In fact, Smith, who would be nicknamed "the Flying Flapper" by the New York media, was already a skilled pilot; she began flying lessons at age 10, Orville Wright himself finalized her pilot's license when she was just 16, and she went on to set numerous altitude records. In September 1928, just one month before her East River adventure, Smith was in the Adirondacks, where she was reported to be scouting for potential landing fields in Lake Placid and Saranac Lake. The *Lake Placid News* later reported that Smith flew her own plane to the Adirondacks. (Courtesy of Leslie Jones Collection, Boston Public Library.)

There are a select few names associated with flying services in the Adirondacks, such as Bird, Payne, and Helms. Born in 1916 in Long Lake, Herb Helms was a lifelong pilot whose company, Helms Aero Service, gave many locals and visitors their first experience of flight and inspired countless postcards of Helms planes attractively parked on the beach in front of the old Hotel Adirondack. He was also called upon to be the pilot who took Gov. Nelson Rockefeller on a flight that landed at the beach in Speculator. This image of the suited governor and the more casually attired pilot is an excellent representation of the friendly, ready-for-adventure Adirondack aviator. (Courtesy of Tim Helms.)

With their tremendous natural beauty and proximity to the major cities of the northeast, it is logical that the Adirondack Mountains, with all their peaks, lakes, and distinctive features, would draw vacationers, including the famous. For every senator or movie star who visits, there are those who do not become famous until later in life, when historians can say, "Yes, that person was here." One such person was aviatrix Amelia Earhart, who captured the attention of the world in the 1920s and 1930s with her groundbreaking feats and eventual disappearance over the South Pacific. Before she was famous, when she was a 22-year-old student, Earhart vacationed with her mother in Lake George, spending six months in a rented cottage, as seen here, with her distinctive short haircut evident. The following year, Earhart took her first flight as a passenger. Thereafter, history was made. (Courtesy of Schlesinger Library, Harvard Radcliffe Institute.)

There is quite a bit of aviation—as well as local—history in this image, which shows, from left to right, Saranac Lake residents Frank Kawatch, Eugene Keet, and Christy Mathewson Jr. Keet and Mathewson were accomplished, adventurous pilots, and Kawatch, who moved to Saranac Lake to "take the cure" for tuberculosis, was a photographer who had a notable, albeit ill-fated, local adventure when sailing with Albert Einstein. In the winter of 1928–1929, Keet and Mathewson offered passenger flights in Saranac Lake; when they leased the airport in Wilmington the following summer, the announcement made the news section of *Aero Digest*, a popular monthly magazine. Throughout his career, Keet also made airplane mail runs, while Mathewson, who had been among the first cadets in the Army Air Corps, saw duty in the Flying Training Command. His father, Christy Mathewson Sr., had moved the family to Saranac Lake to receive treatment for tuberculosis after a Hall of Fame baseball career. (Courtesy of SLFLARR.)

Most Adirondack small towns had at least one photographer whose body of work remains to enlighten following generations on what life was like in that town. For Saranac Lake, that photographer was William Kollecker, whose name is still well-known and whose images—clear and crisp—continue to appear in many books, magazines, and museum exhibits. Here, Kollecker (center) and his assistant Hugo Franz pose with cameras and other photographers on a snowy, cold winter day. The image was likely taken on Lake Flower, the same day as the photograph on page 13, when the photographers captured images of a plane on skis. Throughout his career, Kollecker was an enthusiastic photographer, willing to go anywhere, take scores of photographs, develop them, and offer the prints for sale almost immediately in his Main Street shop. His images of George Gray's historic flight in 1912 are of particular interest and importance. (Courtesy of SLFLARR.)

There is a plaque located at Marcy Field in Keene Valley dedicating the field to Dr. Alphonso Goff, a local legend and deeply beloved by the community, both in his role as a physician and for the color he brought to the area. Dr. Goff (known as "Doc") was the stereotypical country doctor, the sort of man a movie could have easily been made about; he would refuse payment when he knew a patient was struggling and give small gifts to young patients to soothe them. One of Dr. Goff's most well-known traits was his love of speed: both in his Jeep and in the air. It was Dr. Goff who, in 1938, made the first airmail flight in the Adirondacks and who, when stopped by a state trooper for speeding, handed over his pilot's license when the trooper jokingly asked if he had one. He is seen here at the hangar at Marcy Field in front of his Aeronca with its distinctive nose. Doc owned as many as three airplanes at once. (Courtesy of KVL.)

Generous with his time, medical expertise, and kindness, Dr. Goff was happy to talk planes with anyone who was interested. Here, he is in the midst of a crowd of children and adults. One person Dr. Goff erred with when it came to his flying, however, was his mother. Later in life, Doc recalled her being what he called "pecky" one day, and Dr. Goff could not understand why. It turned out that she, at the age of about 80, was hurt that he had not taken her up in his airplane. Dr. Goff promptly took his mother flying and reported that she had a wonderful time. On another occasion, Goff had to land in a farmer's field after trouble with his airplane. The farmer approached him and said simply, "Be you the mail?'" (Courtesy of KVL.)

In 1927, three gentlemen who worked on Wall Street purchased a piece of land in Wilmington as a place to go fly-fishing and get away from the city. One of the men was Joe Patterson, the founder of the *New York Daily News*. His daughter Alicia visited the area with him, a young woman whom he had raised with an interest in adventurous pursuits. Around 1930, Alicia learned to fly alongside her father and began to participate in races, at one point setting a record for a woman pilot flying from New York to Philadelphia. The property in Wilmington became a camp with its own airstrip, one that is still in private hands today, and Alicia flew there amid writing jobs, races, and working as a transport pilot. Later in her life, she would found *Newsday*.

Among other planes—Patterson flew off on her honeymoon with her second husband and their mechanic in a Bellanca monoplane—Alicia Patterson owned and flew a single-engine biplane built by the Laird company, which suited her, as she enjoyed racing and Laird planes were built for speed and high performance. Patterson's Laird LC-R, seen in both of these images, had a Wright Whirlwind engine, could carry the pilot and one passenger, and was evidently one of only two built by Laird. In the image below, the Laird is seen at her father's private airfield in Wilmington. The house pictured was later moved and still stands in Wilmington. (Both, courtesy of Jim Catalano Collection, WHS.)

FATHER SCHULTE & FATHER BARRY LEAVING DONTEN-WILL BEACH. ESSEX, N. Y. ON LAKE CHAMPLAIN

On September 16, 1938, a headline on the front page of the *Essex County Republican* proclaimed, "Flying Priest from Arctic Visits Essex." Known around the world as "the Flying Priest," Paul Schulte was a German Oblate priest who founded an organization, the Missionary International Vehicular Association (MIVA), to provide aircraft and other vehicles to missionaries in remote parts of the world, work inspired by the death of a childhood friend in 1925. Father Schulte said the world's first aerial mass on the *Hindenburg* and, in 1938, flew a daring rescue mission to Arctic Bay on the far northern coast of Canada's Baffin Island, where an ill priest was saved thanks to Father Schulte and his aircraft. Following his 2,200-mile mission to Arctic Bay, Father Schulte visited fellow Oblate Fathers in Essex, parking his Stinson aircraft on the shore of Lake Champlain in front of the order's home. Father Schulte's visit drew crowds, and images taken of the plane were immortalized as postcards. Here, Schulte himself is pictured center.

In the southern Adirondacks, many travelers visiting the Lake George area who have their own planes fly to Floyd Bennett Memorial Airfield in Queensbury. Bennett was an aviator born in what is now the village of Lake George who became a legendary pilot and whose experiences ranged from the Adirondacks to the Arctic. A talented mechanic, Bennett joined the Navy as a young man, became a pilot, and there befriended fellow aviator Richard Byrd. Together, the two men would go on to make historic expeditions to the Arctic, including a flight to the North Pole. Although Bennett would be awarded the Congressional Medal of Honor, he remained humble and close to his Adirondack roots, regularly returning to the places he had grown up: Lake George and Ticonderoga, where he was popular, with local papers referring to him as "one of our own boys." (Courtesy of Library of Congress.)

In 1925, Bennett was chosen to serve with Byrd on an expedition to Greenland. The adventure was a dangerous one, in which Bennett saved both men's lives through his skill and quick thinking. This mission was followed by the expedition that made both men world-famous: a flight to the North Pole. This image shows the aircraft Bennett and Byrd flew, a Fokker trimotor named *Josephine Ford*, when the aviators were in Spitsbergen, preparing to depart for the pole. In a flight lasting 15 hours and 57 minutes, Byrd and Bennett flew to the pole and returned to Spitsbergen. Following this tremendous success, Byrd and Bennett prepared for an ambitious journey to the South Pole. Part of their preparations involved testing the skis their plane was fitted with; Bennett chose to practice on the mostly frozen Lake Champlain, near his home of Ticonderoga. His return to the village was met with great excitement and everywhere he went, he was treated as a hero. Sadly, Bennett died while on a rescue mission but is still well remembered in the Adirondacks for his brilliant aviation career. (Courtesy of Library of Congress.)

Known as "the Adirondack hermit," Noah John Rondeau lived alone in the wilderness of Cold River for two decades, though he was a welcoming character who did not shun visitors, played the violin, and kept extensive journals of his life in the wild (although many of his writings were in a complex cipher). A skilled hunter and trapper, Rondeau lived at Coreys, near Tupper Lake, for many years before moving to Cold River, where he proclaimed himself mayor of the settlement with its population of one. Yet Rondeau did emerge from the woods on occasion, such as seen here in 1947, when he was plucked from his isolated home by a helicopter and flown to Manhattan for an appearance at the National Sportsmen's Show, the first of several such public appearances. Rondeau's outing in 1947 was recorded in this image, taken at the Saranac Lake Airport. (Courtesy of SLFLARR.)

Despite his reputation as a hermit, Noah John Rondeau did occasionally venture out of Cold River, picked up by plane by Herb Helms to go shopping for supplies or to visit friends. In 1948, at the age of 64, Rondeau took on an adventure by taking a flying lesson in Lake Placid, which was given to him by Patricia Houran Rideout. Rideout ran a flying service and school at the Lake Placid Airport with her husband, Harold; previously, Rideout had been a member of the Women's Airforce Service Pilots (WASP) organization. As a WASP, Rideout trained at Avenger Field, pictured here, becoming a flight instructor for both male and female pilots. In addition to the flight school in Lake Placid, Rideout was also a pilot examiner. Later in life, she, along with the other WASPs, was awarded the Congressional Gold Medal and veteran status, something previously denied to them. (Courtesy of TWU.)

Billing himself as "The Flying Photographer," Canton resident Dwight Church ran an extensive business combining photography and aviation. In addition to his "Skyview" postcards, Church also found success in photographing local farms for area residents, who were delighted to have expansive, unique views of their farms. (Courtesy of Lamar Bliss.)

Already a young photographer with a motorcycle, Church took his first flying lessons in 1928 and quickly purchased his first plane. Church took many of his photographs from this plane, which he dubbed "Love Nest," although it is not clear why it earned that name. The "Love Nest" was a Monosport Model 2, a two-seater. (Courtesy of Lamar Bliss.)

40

Above Tupper Lake, Lake Simonds and Whiteface Mt.
(Skyview by Dwight Church)

The Flying Photographer provided many images of the Adirondacks as they were in the early to mid-20th century. Located in Tupper Lake, Lake Simond is essentially a floodplain of the Raquette River, which flows north to the St. Lawrence. In 1858, Ralph Waldo Emerson and friends paddled the Raquette River, a trip that Emerson immortalized in the poem "The Adirondacs." The party paddled these very waters.

Dwight Church (The Flying Photographer) No. 7765.

Known for asking farmers "How'd you like to see your farm as God sees it?" and offering aerial photographs, Church also gave a number of free rides in his airplanes, such as in this Piper, as well as advertised free flights (with photograph packages) in October to enjoy the colors of fall. The flights were particularly advertised to those interested in flying and aviation. (Courtesy of Lamar Bliss.)

Born in Harrietstown, Mary Elizabeth Pettitt grew up on the shores of Upper Saranac Lake, in the historic hamlet of Saranac Inn. As a young woman, a flight on a DC-3 passenger plane from Montreal to New York caused her to fall in love with flying, and it was shortly thereafter that Pettitt learned about the Women's Airforce Service Pilots (WASP) program, which she was determined to join, getting her pilot's license in order to qualify. WASPs did not see combat, but they were an instrumental part of the war effort, flying planes to where they were needed, training other pilots, towing gunnery targets, and more. After the war, Pettitt remained a pilot, working as a skywriter and a copilot for a private airline. She held WASP reunions at Saranac Inn, and she was a great supporter of their history and place in aviation history. (Both, courtesy of TWU.)

Three

ADVENTURES IN THE WILDERNESS

During the 20th century, adventures in the Adirondack wilderness were a colorful mixture of old and new, as seen in this image, where two men in a canoe, the craft replete with gear and supplies, pass by a modern floatplane. Rather than take over, floatplanes made wilderness adventures more accessible, and more than one canoe traveled to the woods via plane. (Courtesy of TOWHA.)

The packbasket is a ubiquitous Adirondack accessory, seen on the backs of hikers, sportsmen, and adventurers for over a century. Although many contemporary hikers choose high-tech backpacks, there are many who continue to show their loyalty to the humble packbasket. Usually made of black ash, the traditional packbasket may have been inspired by the carrying baskets of the indigenous people of the area. The men embarking on an adventure via a Phoenix Air Service plane (pilot and owner Merrill Phoenix is seen at the rear of the group) may have chosen a modern form of transport, but the packbaskets carrying their gear speak to an earlier time when many guides relied on the baskets for their lightweight, splinter-free qualities. (Courtesy of TOWHA.)

One of the longest-lasting floatplane businesses in the Adirondacks, Payne's Air Service on Seventh Lake in Inlet is a service that has been run by the same family for generations, despite changes in tourism, the economy, and even the regulations surrounding motorized craft on Adirondack lakes. More than 50 years ago, pilot Jim Payne started his business, transporting fishermen, hunters, photographers, and other outdoorsmen and women throughout the southern Adirondacks. There was a time when there were fewer restrictions on where floatplanes could land, making much of the Adirondacks open to wilderness adventure. Despite increased limits, the Payne family has continued to introduce families and children to their aerial playground on short scenic jaunts as well as repeat adventurers who rely on them to carry them safely to adventure. (Courtesy of HCH.)

Unlike traditional airports and airfields, floatplanes offer pilots and their passengers the ability to land in a variety of unique locations, such as town beaches. This snapshot from the Speculator beach shows just how easily floatplanes could get to town centers. While the planes on the beach would certainly draw an interested crowd, this image may have been taken on the day of Governor Rockefeller's visit. (Courtesy of HCH.)

Floatplanes were not used simply for getting to remote areas, they also became fixtures of excitement at lakeside resorts and small towns. Otter Lake, located west of Old Forge, is a charming hamlet that was the site of a large hotel until 1946. The hotel boasted of having the best deer hunting in the Adirondacks, which would have drawn more than one hunter via floatplane.

Started in the 19th century by several businessmen from locations throughout the state of New York, the Rap-Shaw Club still welcomes members and their guests to tranquil, classic Adirondack getaways. Originally located on Burnt Lake, the club moved to two islands in Stillwater Reservoir, itself tucked away amid the lands of the Independence River Wild Forest and the Five Ponds Wilderness, in the 1940s. The club is only accessible by water, but even before the move to the island, floatplanes were in use by the club. This plane, a Stinson SM-2AC (or Stinson Junior) was owned by the Central Adirondack Aviation Corporation and used by the Rap-Shaw Club to stock fish. It has been said that this Stinson was the first aircraft to be equipped with Fairchild floats in lieu of wheels and was a busy plane throughout the Eagle Bay area. (Courtesy of TOWHA.)

Phoenix Adirondack Flights was a business that operated in Inlet at the Wood Hotel, now known as the Woods Inn. Phoenix was owned and operated by Merrill Phoenix, a local aviator who started flying at the age of 18. Like many early, eager pilots, Phoenix received flying instruction in exchange for helping out around the hangar, where he developed a natural mechanical brilliance and became a pilot of distinction and fine ability. Phoenix was known for his horseshoe-shaped takeoffs on small—too small for many pilots—sites such as Beaver Lake and for his gentle landings that were akin to a leaf falling: a descent without a lot of forward motion. Phoenix, who gradually lost his hearing thanks to so much time in open cockpits, also flew patients in need of medical care to local hospitals, flew in World War II, and attempted a light aircraft record for time aloft in 1938. (Courtesy of TOWHA.)

In the 19th and early 20th centuries, adventures in the Adirondack backcountry were plentiful but required considerable effort and resources. The introduction of the floatplane changed that; suddenly, fishermen, hunters, and campers could be flown into the wilderness along with supplies and then just as easily flown out, perhaps with game in tow. This made the process of getting to the wilderness faster as well, as compared to the days in which it was necessary to undertake an extensive paddle to reach one's destination. In this image from the 1940s, pilot Merrill Phoenix stands on the dock while a gentleman by the name of Henry Nortz emerges from the plane, helping to unload several cases of Genesee beer and other supplies from a seaplane operated by Phoenix's company, Phoenix Adirondack Flights. The bow of what may be a guideboat peeks into the frame on the lower right, hinting at promising adventures ahead. (Courtesy of TOWHA.)

The Fulton Chain of Lakes is a stretch of waterways surrounded by vast expanses of forest, habitat for moose, and ideal for floatplane businesses and adventures. For several decades, the Bald Mountain House operated on Third Lake, near the towns of Old Forge and Inlet. Amid the cottages, sports, and taproom, the main building overlooked the lake and a distinctive craft tied to the dock: a Curtiss Robin floatplane, serving as the local air taxi. Since their inception, Curtiss Robins have been reliable aircraft. Floatplanes like the air taxi made getting from a hotel to an excursion, from one lake to another, or to explore other towns as easy as walking from the hotel to the dock. During the 1930s, several air taxi services operated in the Adirondacks as well as in surrounding areas, such as Plattsburgh-Burlington. (Courtesy of TOWHA.)

Aviators in the Adirondacks have always had to be versatile: jobs, calls, and even favors might have come in asking for anything from a nighttime flight to bring a doctor to a quiet spot on an emergency case or delivering cans of fish to remote lakes to ferrying well-heeled summer residents to their Great Camps or picking up hunters after a week of sport. One of the best, called upon to do all of that and more, was Harold Scott of Inlet, known to all as "Scotty." Scotty (left, with Stubby Weedmark) took to flying from an early age, saving up for flight school and purchasing a World War I surplus plane, which he flew over his mother's home. Once in Inlet, Scotty proved adept at tricky landings on tiny lakes and was known as the first man in the Adirondacks to land a floatplane on a frozen lake. Scotty was known by many other pilots in the Adirondacks as among the very best; Herb Helms in Long Lake greatly admired the older pilot and coveted rides in his plane. (Courtesy of TOWHA.)

This early, sepia-toned aerial photograph shows a tranquil view of Lake Placid's Mirror Lake in the foreground, while the village's namesake lake is visible to the left. Dominating the view of all is Whiteface Mountain, which lies just a few miles northeast of the village. On the point of land between the lakes lies Stevens House, one of Lake Placid's most famous former resorts. (Courtesy of SLFLARR.)

With aviation came a new way to advertise, as in this advertisement in which the lakeside Stevens House is shown to advantage in an aerial photograph. For a few decades, Stevens House was one of the premier hotels in the Adirondacks, drawing guests for luxurious summer relaxation and access to the nearby High Peaks. Although successful, the hotel did not survive the 1929 stock market crash and was ultimately demolished.

Different from a floatplane, hydroplanes are more akin to a flying boat; in fact, that is the correct term, thanks to the fact that the hydroplane lands on its specialized hull, rather than pontoons. Hydroplanes were seen on Lake George as early as 1921; this card was postmarked June 15, 1925. Nowadays, a hydroplane most often refers to a boat that skims the surface of the water at great speed.

WEST END OF THE PERGOLA, LOOKING TOWARD THE VILLAGE, LAKE GEORGE, N. Y. 242

With thousands of lakes and ponds in the Adirondacks, the seaplane has long been incredibly popular in the area, particularly in Lake George. In this early illustrated postcard of the Pergola Casino at the Fort William Henry Hotel, several planes are seen parked on the lakeshore. Local marinas and seaplane bases, such as Hall's, offered scenic flights as well as flying instruction.

Located on Fourth Lake, Minnowbrook Resort featured cottages in a pine forest, swimming, boating, and other forms of summer relaxation. In advertising a "homelike atmosphere" in its clubhouse and the scenery of the namesake brook, the resort offered classic charm. The arrival of a floatplane, as seen in this image from 1934, would surely have generated more modern excitement. (Courtesy of ADKX.)

The largest in the Fulton Chain of Lakes, Fourth Lake, and the communities of Inlet and Eagle Bay have a long and wonderful aviation history—and a well-documented one, at that. Whether travelers took a scenic flight or merely spotted attractive floatplanes at the ready, a postcard such as this made a fine souvenir.

Built in 1901, the Osborne Inn occupied a point of land on Lake Pleasant in Speculator, close to where the Sacandaga River flows into the lake. Osborne's was ideally situated next to the beach, as Lake Pleasant itself has long been a vacation destination, particularly for those with floatplanes. Although it, like so many other sprawling Adirondack hotels, would ultimately be demolished, the Osborne Inn gained some fame for being the site of a terrific boxing training camp. Bill Osborne, son of the owners William and Nora Osborne, was a decorated World War I hero and cornerman who encouraged his friend, boxer Gene Tunney, to train in Speculator. This led to other boxers making their way to Speculator, where training matches were watched by enthusiastic crowds amid Osborne and Speculator's scenic beauty. Thanks to Lake Pleasant's size and ideal southern Adirondacks location, floatplanes have been a regular feature on the lake for decades, and it is still the site of an annual fly-in that draws many vintage aircraft. (Courtesy of HCH.)

Abrams Piseco Lake

Legend has it that for a time, Abram's in Piseco, which had a floatplane hangar, offered short hops to overnight guests in a floatplane, but such trips were cut short when the plane was set ablaze by vandals. Because the flights were so popular and such a novel way to experience the Adirondacks, owner Bill Abrams immediately set out to purchase another plane. This floatplane, built by the WACO Aircraft Company, was the replacement Abrams purchased. Not only would this WACO CSO delight guests, but it would go on to have a long and prosperous life. Built in 1930, the plane has been outfitted with both wheels and floats in the course of its long history and was piloted by a number of notable local aviators for charters, sightseeing flights, and even fish planting. Remarkably, the plane still flies and, despite having had a few owners since the 1930s, has even returned to Piseco, where it was reunited with many who had flown it long ago. (Courtesy of Frederick and Cynthia Adcock, *Piseco Lake and Arietta*.)

Located on the eastern end of Piseco Lake in the southwestern Adirondacks, Pine Island has long been an easily accessible destination for summer visitors in nearby Piseco, offering scenic views and pretty spots for a summer picnic. The arrival of a biplane floatplane on the shore, adjacent to a more traditional style of transportation in the form of a guideboat, would have justifiably drawn a crowd. In the image, the pilot may be seen standing next to the plane, while a passenger, most likely a woman based on the draped clothing, stands on the wing. Aviator George Gray often found he had to keep his plane guarded or under cover, so often was his plane damaged by curious onlookers snipping off bits of the canvas that covered the wings. This group of summer adventurers of all ages seems content to merely watch the goings on. (Courtesy of Frederick and Cynthia Adcock, *Piseco Lake and Arietta*.)

Throughout the 1940s and 1950s, the Windhausen brothers, Matthew and Charles, better known respectively as "Bud" and "Chuck," flew the Eagle Bay area, their base a simple dirt drive loop, seen here with one of the Windhausen planes at the dock near the Eagle Bay Hotel. The Windhausens opened their business after Harold Scott retired, and the pair enjoyed adventures in their WACO biplanes. (Courtesy of TOWHA.)

Looking closely, one of the Windhausen brothers can be seen at the controls of a WACO flying over Eagle Bay, their company name, Adirondack Airlines, visible on the door. The brothers had many successes in the area, although another WACO belonging to the brothers, which they used for winter flights, was damaged in a rescue flight. (Courtesy of TOWHA.)

The opportunity that the many air service businesses in the Adirondacks offered people, to get up in the air for a brief but exceptional ride at an affordable price, led to many first flights. A girl camper sent this postcard home from Long Lake, remarking, "We finally did it—went flying in this ski plane. We went for a 15 min ride."

Although many illustrated postcards of the Adirondacks—or anyplace, for that matter—may show an idealized view from the air, this postcard, claiming to show the view from 4,500 feet up, helps illustrate just why Long Lake got its name. Measuring 14 miles long, the lakeshore is largely undeveloped, even to this day.

Now legendary in the Long Lake area, Helms Aero Service got its start in 1947 when the three Helms brothers—Herb, Eddie, and Gib—banded together after World War II to start their own business. During the war, Gib and Herb had both flown in B-24 Liberator bombers, with Gib as a pilot and Herb as a navigator. After a few years, Gib decided to sell his share to Herb, and Eddie did as well after ending up in a tree. Herb grew the business from there. Despite its size, Long Lake has but one small stretch of water that is crossed by motorists, and it is there at the beach that Helms Aero Service has taken off for more than 70 years, with scenic flights, charters, help with fire spotting, delivery of goods, searches for missing planes, and picking up travelers both famous and infamous. Just as Herb was inspired by Harold Scott, he, in turn, inspired generations of local Adirondack aviators, from kids who got their first flight from Herb to his own family. (Courtesy of Tim Helms.)

Like his father before him, Tom Helms became a legendary pilot in his own right. Following a distinguished career in the military and a degree in mathematics, Tom, who passed away in 2022, became a crucial part of Helms Aero Service and the Long Lake community, first partnering with his father, Herb, and then taking over after Herb's death, carrying on what many view as a Long Lake institution, through government hurdles and changes in the kind of flights customers were looking for. Tom's skills as a pilot, and his keen knowledge of the landscape, were especially crucial in the decades when environmental impacts such as acid rain came to the fore and scientists sought time in the skies. (Courtesy of Tim Helms.)

Most flying services try to close up shop and tuck the planes in during fall, but the notoriously unpredictable Adirondack weather sometimes has other plans in store. Snow may arrive just about any time after mid-September. This image, a favorite in the Helms family, captures a Helms Aero Service plane landing amid a fresh dusting of snow—a scene that may have been even more impressive for the pilot and passengers. (Courtesy of Tim Helms.)

Helms Aero Service has been in operation for 76 years and is now run by its third generation. Following Tom's death in 2022, his son, also named Tom, took over the controls as a pilot. He is seen here on the shores of Long Lake with his father and grandfather. (Courtesy of Tim Helms.)

This vintage advertisement for Bud Windhausen's seaplane flights appeared in the *Adirondack Arrow*, a weekly newspaper that covered the news in and around Old Forge and Inlet. The advertisement appeared in the *Arrow* on May 8, 1954. Both Windhausen brothers lived in houses on the grounds of the Eagle Bay Hotel, within easy reach of their base of operations. (Courtesy of TOWHA.)

America's Finest All-Metal Seaplane

FLY WITH *Bud Windhausen*

SEAPLANE BASE — EAGLE BAY, N. Y.

Scenic -:- Charter -:- Fishing -:- Hunting

For Service — Call Eagle Bay 2861

Located on a particularly cobbled bit of land extending into Fourth Lake, Rocky Point was the site of the similarly named Rocky Point Hotel, an establishment that opened in the late 1800s, although success was slow to start. Initially consisting of guest rooms with no bathrooms, the hotel developed through a series of owners and saw the addition of cottages, tennis courts, and many of the amenities that typified the finer Adirondack hotels. In the heyday of floatplanes, sightseeing rides were offered. The plane seen here at the dock is a WACO seaplane that belonged to Merrill Phoenix; his logo of a stylized bird can be seen on the fuselage. The plane, now outfitted with wheels instead of floats, is on display at the New England Air Museum in Hartford, Connecticut. (Courtesy of TOWHA.)

At a dock on Big Moose Lake, northwest of Old Forge, the Eagle Bay Stinson, which belonged to the Central Adirondack Aviation Corporation and made many memorable flights around the area and throughout the Adirondacks, waits for its next flight. It is said that the Stinson had a rear seat made of wicker, providing passengers with a comfortable ride. (Courtesy of TOWHA.)

Located northwest of Eagle Bay in the Fulton Chain Wild Forest, Moss Lake has long been a picturesque spot, especially viewed from above. This postcard by photographer Henry Beach captures the wilderness, which attracted youngsters when the lake was home to a girl's camp. In the 1970s, Mohawks from Kahnawake and Akwesasne moved into the property, reclaiming ancestral lands. Today, the lake is still just as attractive. (Courtesy of ADKX.)

With Adirondack weather so changeable, adventurers have to make do and adapt as best they can. A sudden, quick freeze at Bear Pond, located deep within the Moose River Plains Wild Forest, caused a group of hunters to decamp and move their game (seen in the background, hanging from the trees) to Beaver River Flow one by one. Harold "Scotty" Scott was the pilot who helped the hunters, his plane outfitted with skis for a frozen landing. Scotty was a terrific pilot to have around in a pinch, though not all of his passengers always realized it. An older passenger on a sightseeing flight once cracked Scotty over the head with her purse when she thought he was asleep at the controls. Rather, Scotty had his eyes closed to listen to the engine. (Courtesy of TOWHA.)

With so many remote camps and lodges scattered throughout the park, many of them difficult to reach in any season, repairs and building projects take place whenever possible, even in the chill of winter. In this undated photograph, a truck from the George Deis lumber mill stands by a Windhausen brothers' plane for a presumed delivery. (Courtesy of TOWHA.)

With its hangar at Big Moose, Philip Ellsworth's Adirondack Air Service operated year-round, albeit part-time. Ellsworth ran the company in part for business but also because he enjoyed flying and offering instruction. Ellsworth had grown up going to Big Moose in summers with his parents and found the area ideal for flying hunting groups, including his friends. (Courtesy of TOWHA.)

th Range from above Cascade Mt.
(Skyview © by Dwight Church)

Almost as soon as there were planes in the Adirondacks, there were aerial photographs of the landscape. Canton native Dwight Church's Photo Park Studio sold postcards of his "Skyview" images, such as this one of the High Peaks. To take effective photographs, Church modified an early Kodak Autographic folding camera with a special viewfinder; his camera is now in the collection at the Adirondack Experience: The Museum on Blue Mountain Lake.

BIRD'S-EYE VIEW OF OLD FORGE, N. Y., ADIRONDACK MTS., FROM AIRPLANE AT 4000 FT.   285

(C) 707 STANDARD SUPPLY CO., OTTER LAKE, N. Y.

With Old Forge and the surrounding area so much a part of Adirondack aviation history, it seems fitting that an aerial view of the town should be shared on these pages. This hand-colored photograph view, which was printed and sold by the Standard Supply Company in Otter Lake, shows Old Forge prior to the 1950s, when Enchanted Forest was built.

An important part of life in the village of Saranac Lake and providing year-round recreation, Lake Flower was created in 1827 by the construction of a dam across the Saranac River. Since the early years of aviation, the lake has been an excellent location for landing, whether on the water in warm weather or ice in winter. The homes in the background are a clue to the location: all three homes seen on the hillside beyond the lake are still in existence, with many of the same features intact and clearly recognizable. The home on the far right was once a private tuberculosis sanatorium; the sight of floatplanes landing on the lake from the porches must have been an exciting sight for patients, many of whom were largely confined to their cure cottages and fresh air sleeping porches. (Courtesy of SLFLARR.)

Before the creation of the Adirondack Park Agency and the many initiatives to protect Adirondack waters, floatplanes could land on just about any lake or pond the pilot felt compelled to attempt. Some pilots throughout the region became well known for their highly adept handling of floatplanes on small bodies of water that did not allow for much space to take off or land. Because of the agency's changes, floatplanes are seen on far fewer lakes and ponds than in the past. This biplane floatplane, moving at a speedy pace on Lake Flower, would have given onlookers a good show. (Courtesy of SLFLARR.)

A winter flight offered the unidentified pilot and photographer of this image the opportunity to view downtown Saranac Lake's unique buildings, from the formidable bulk of the redbrick Hotel Saranac at the right to the small cluster of churches located at the center. Today, this pre-1958 image offers a glimpse of Saranac Lake in a quieter time, without the current highway that crosses the Saranac River. (Courtesy of SLFLARR.)

While many things in Adirondack towns change from year to year, the mountains themselves remain steadfast. In this undated image taken above Saranac Lake, McKenzie Mountain looms in the left of the image, while Cascade sits at the center, past Lake Placid to the southeast. The mountains and their rough, unpredictable weather have long been a challenge to aviators. (Courtesy of SLFLARR.)

Perhaps a souvenir of a flight, or perhaps simply a snapshot capturing a moment when a plane was unexpectedly encountered, this photograph of an unidentified woman is a reminder of a time when air travel was still novel, exciting, and something to pose for a photograph over. Dated October 12, 1930, this image appears to show the Travel Air floatplane kept at Abram's resort on Piseco Lake. Perhaps the woman in the photograph enjoyed a ride in the plane while at Abram's or was excited simply to be near the gleaming aircraft. Either way, the snapshot captures the joy that the floatplanes of the Adirondacks have been bringing to people for over a century. (Courtesy of HCH.)

Adirondack lakes are not always known for their calm days, and despite the fact that floatplanes are designed to operate only up to a certain wave height, days as calm as this may look serene, but they are actually among the most dangerous for pilots, perhaps offering a reason why the planes are parked. Although Adirondack aviators are known for their daring, exceptional skills, and ability to pilot in any weather, they are also generally wise and seasoned. For non-pilots, the image of the two planes, their reflections on water as clear as glass, is a scenic reminder of the beauty of flight in the Adirondacks and the opportunities it brings to experience the wilderness in a new way. (Courtesy of HCH.)

Four

SERVICE AND INDUSTRY

Throughout the 20th century, a variety of aircraft were pressed into service not simply for adventure, but for service as well. A Phoenix Air Services floatplane is seen on the shore of Brandreth Lake, a preserve in Hamilton County that is the oldest family-owned preserve in the state, with milk cans for transporting fish alongside. (Courtesy of TOWHA.)

As the Adirondacks increasingly opened up to tourism and as a vacation destination for adventurers, the natural environment was therefore impacted. Among other species, brook trout numbers declined as the wilderness was increasingly fished; stocking fish from hatcheries was the solution, but getting the fish to the right areas was problematic. By the 1930s, however, a novel solution was found: floatplanes carrying cans of fingerling trout traveled from hatcheries to remote lakes and ponds, where the fry were released, a prelude to later adventures in which the fish were dropped from a very low altitude via tanks in the plane. (Above, courtesy of Historic Saranac Lake Collection [2022.144.173.5]; below, courtesy of TOWHA.)

Originally from Chateaugay in northern Franklin County, Carl Prue, seen here with snowshoes and packbasket next to an aircraft on skis, was a longtime New York state conservation officer. During his time with what is now known as the Department of Environmental Conservation (DEC), Prue worked as a game protector, monitoring wildlife numbers and investigating incidents and accidents involving wildlife at a variety of locations. Prue retired as head of the DEC's law enforcement division and was considered an expert on wildlife and forest management. Here, he is on duty with an unidentified pilot at Schroon Lake in the 1940s. Aircraft have long been used by conservation officers to monitor wildlife and conduct counts of specific species such as beaver and moose. (Courtesy of Historic Saranac Lake Collection [2022.144.59].)

Located amid the depths of what is now the Five Ponds Wilderness Area, a part of the Adirondacks covering more than 100,000 acres, Crooked Lake is an isolated, yet beautiful spot known for excellent fishing in Herkimer County. Yet Crooked Lake, like so many other bodies of water in the Adirondacks, has seen periods of low numbers. This image from the 1940s shows the cabin plane owned by Merrill Phoenix being utilized at Crooked Lake to plant fish via the traditional method of recycled milk cans. The man on the right may be Dennis Hartnett, a member of the Rap-Shaw Club who hired Phoenix to deliver cans of fish to a number of lakes, which he did over the course of several flights. (Courtesy of TOWHA.)

Merrill Phoenix was not the only aviator in the Adirondacks to be involved with fish stocking and a variety of jobs of service to the state. Starting in the 1940s, Seaplane Airways out of Speculator, which owned and operated the WACO floatplane seen here, had a number of jobs it undertook for the state; in addition to fish stocking, Seaplane hauled supplies to locations where ranger stations were to be constructed, transported food for workers at remote sites, and transported a number of state employees, including at least one group of firefighters headed to Beaver Lake. One of the pilots for Seaplane was Charlie Smith, who, among other flights, flew boxer Max Schmeling to the training camp at Osborne's in Speculator. (Courtesy of HCH.)

A pilot from Helms Aero Service captured this image of the fire tower on Kempshall Mountain near Long Lake. The summit once held this fire tower, a steel structure used for spotting wildfires. Eventually, the tower was deemed unnecessary and dismantled. It does, however, live on at the Adirondack History Museum in Elizabethtown, where a tower is on display, made in part from pieces of the Kempshall Tower. (Courtesy of Tim Helms.)

In addition to using aircraft for wildlife surveys, forest fire watches, and other environmental concerns, the state of New York also used aircraft for a controversial period during which chemicals were dispersed over the landscape in an attempt to eliminate pests such as black flies. Here, a Bell helicopter is prepared by a pilot alongside state entomologist Dr. Hugh Glasgow. (Courtesy of TOWHA.)

Early in the 20th century, New York state officials were quick to see the benefits of utilizing aircraft for a range of uses in the backcountry, as this image demonstrates. Preserved by the late DEC forest ranger Franklin Wheeler, who served as a conservation officer from 1946 to 1971 out of Warrensburg, this image shows a biplane spraying an unknown material on the ground below. Throughout his career, Ranger Wheeler was active in working on summit fire towers as well as fighting fires. Although Adirondack summits were once home to observers in fire towers watching for a hint of fire, airplanes gradually became the preferred method for watching for as well as fighting potentially devastating forest fires. It is said that Clarence Petty was the first pilot to use a plane to dump water on a forest fire in the Adirondacks. (Courtesy of ADKX.)

A bit of mystery surrounds this photograph, which is in the collection at the Saranac Lake Free Library's Adirondack Research Room. For some time, all three men were unidentified, but it now seems likely that the man on the left is local photographer Frank Kawatch. During the early 20th century, several local garages and numerous individuals in the region had their own planes and were mechanically inclined, with some even going into business, the most notable being the Gladd brothers in Saranac Lake. Lee, Monroe, and Dick Gladd owned and operated an auto dealership in the village that they turned into a defense plant for aircraft parts during World War II. Regardless, the men in this photograph are working on a nine-cylinder aircraft engine, and perhaps the mystery of who they were or what they were working on will be uncovered someday. (Courtesy of SLFLARR.)

In 1924, Sunmount Veterans Administration Hospital opened on former farmland in Tupper Lake as a place to care for veterans who were disabled, injured in World War I, and those suffering from tuberculosis. Many of those with lung ailments who did not have tuberculosis had been gassed and suffered from chronic illness thereafter. Over the years, many of the patients at Sunmount were aviators from World Wars I and II. In the 1960s, Sunmount was also the site of civil defense exercises, which brought thousands of service members and volunteers to the town, an event that drew the attention of the *New York Times* to the small village and hospital. (Courtesy of SLFLARR.)

PALMER-SIMPSON COMPANY

AND AFFILIATED ORGANIZATIONS

are prepared to manufacture
for the United States or
Allied Governments

150 PONTOONS PER MONTH
for hydroaeroplanes, seaplanes and flying boats.

PALMER-SIMPSON CO.

Saranac Lake, N. Y.

The start of World War I brought Saranac Lake into the war effort in a fascinating way: the Palmer-Simpson Company, created by two tuberculosis patients, designed and built hulls and pontoons for 32-foot Curtiss hydroplanes, or flying boats, for the US Navy. Led by Carl Palmer and Dwight Simpson, the company employed just shy of 100 men at the company's two factories in the village. The men employed were mechanics and local boatbuilders, experts in the field of crafting the hulls which were, out of necessity, lightweight. Today, the exact downtown location of the Palmer-Simpson workshops in Saranac Lake is unknown. This advertisement was placed in *Flying* magazine in 1917, but by the end of 1918, production at the factory had ceased due to lack of demand, the US Navy having all the materials and parts it needed.

In this undated World War I–era photograph, the Palmer-Simpson Company displays an example of the aircraft it was helping to build in a parade through downtown Saranac Lake. The flying boat was displayed with the wings significantly shortened, partially in deference to the width of the street. These flying boats had a wingspan of just over 74 feet, yet were built for only a crew of two or three. At a time when many local young men were overseas or in training to go, the display of the Palmer-Simpson contribution, along with the fact that the hulls were made in Saranac Lake, was a source of patriotic local pride. Note the (presumably fake) machine gun on the nose of the plane. Parades in Saranac Lake have long been a community highlight, at holidays and during the annual Winter Carnival. (Courtesy of SLFLARR.)

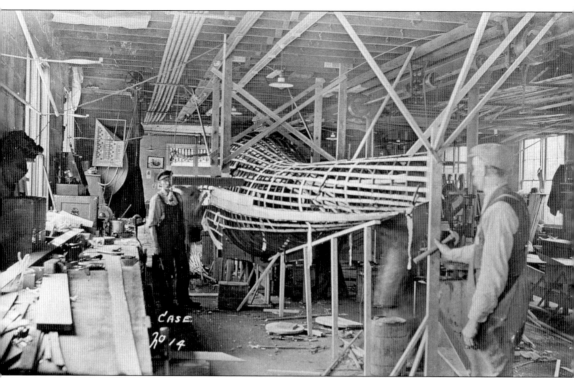

In central New York, monoplane hulls—as well as complete planes—were also built at the Curtiss Aeroplane and Motor factory. The Curtiss company was founded in Hammondsport, near Keuka Lake, in 1909 by Glenn Curtiss, an early aviator who started his career with bicycle racing, then quickly shifted to motorcycles and airplanes. Curtiss developed a number of experimental aircraft and engines, at one point partnering with Alexander Graham Bell in the Aerial Experiment Association. Curtiss not only flew the planes he designed, but he also competed in them, even besting pilots racing in aircraft built by Wilbur and Orville Wright. The Curtiss company eventually had extensive contracts with the US government, including the building of what would be officially known as the Curtiss HS-2L flying boat. This image of a Curtiss workshop, where the flying boat *America* was being built, hints at what the Palmer-Simpson factory may have looked like. (Courtesy of GHCM.)

Thanks to the hard work of the mechanics and boatbuilders employed at the Palmer-Simpson Company in downtown Saranac Lake as well as the many others at the Curtiss Aeroplane and Motor factory in central New York, the US Army Air Service eventually operated upwards of 80 of the HS-2L model flying boats. Following the conclusion of World War I, two of the flying boats were donated to the government of Canada, and several remained in Europe, where they were sold or scrapped. There were so many surplus HS-2Ls left that a number were sold to private individuals and aircraft companies without their engines, giving them a new life, including as bush planes in remote areas. Other HS-2Ls became the property of the US Coast Guard, which used the aircraft at coastal air stations. (Courtesy of USNHHC.)

Which of your neighbors is watching over *your* child tonight?

Tonight—every night—in your town, your state, all over the country thousands of patient, patriotic Americans are serving as civilian plane spotters—guarding against surprise attack from above. This "Sky Watch" is absolutely vital to give warning of hostile aircraft trying to sneak through our radar.

Today the men and women who wear the silver wings of the Ground Observer Corps are doing a job that calls for twice their number. They need more help—*your* help—for *just a few hours a week.* Which of your neighbors is watching over *your* child tonight? *And which night will you guard his?*

Keep your eye on the sky in the

GROUND OBSERVER CORPS

JOIN TODAY — CONTACT CIVIL DEFENSE

PHONE 499

Contributed as a Public Service by

Wake Up!
Sign Up!
Look Up!

Adirondack National Bank & Trust Co.

SARANAC LAKE, NEW YORK

During World War II and the Cold War, the threat of enemy aircraft over American skies was at a new peak. As a result, and with a wish to help protect the public, the Ground Observer Corps was established. In all, more than 1.5 million civilian observers watched the skies at specific observation posts, including in downtown Saranac Lake. This advertisement ran in the *Adirondack Daily Enterprise*.

Patriotism during World War II extended to toy shops in the Adirondacks, which would have carried model planes such as these, made by Cleveland Models. During the war, tuberculosis patients in Saranac Lake were active in building model planes, of American aircraft and of the enemy as well, part of a large-scale effort to familiarize ground observers with the aircraft and also for training purposes.

In Saranac Lake, the roof of the Hotel Saranac became the site of a Ground Observer Corps observation tower, and many locals volunteered to become observers. The tower on the hotel roof was manned by local men who phoned in any aircraft sightings to the correct authorities. It was while on his post that Al Keough spotted a bomber, which turned out to be piloted by his own son Charlie, and raced off to make the important call. At least one local girl, Natalie Bombard Leduc, later recalled delivering meals to her father while he was on post. In the 1950s, a new tower was built elsewhere in the village to watch for planes during Skywatch, the Ground Observer Corps program that took place during the Cold War. Eventually, many local children played on that tower when not in use, and it was subsequently dismantled. (Courtesy of SLFLARR.)

For less than 20 years, the Kinner Airplane & Motor Corp. manufactured aircraft engines, many of which were used in light aircraft and in military trainers. Kinner also produced its own aircraft, including the Kinner Sportster, seen here. The aviator in the photograph may be Saranac Lake resident Charles Keough, who memorably—and infamously—flew a bomber on a training flight to Lake Clear, alarming more than one resident, including his own father, who was stationed in the Hotel Saranac observation tower at the time. During World War II, Keough qualified as an aviator but was largely kept out of the pilot's seat due to an inner ear problem. His foray in the training flight of the bomber made for a long-lasting, and very humorous, story throughout the village, thanks to Keough's gumption and his father's colorful language. On the ground, Keough was an exceptional mechanic and restorer of vintage boats. (Courtesy of SLFLARR.)

Although not within the scope of the Adirondack Park itself, the US Army military reservation of Fort Drum has long played a role in what flies over Adirondack skies. What is now known as Fort Drum began as an encampment named Pine Camp in 1908, as a site for Army training purposes. The site grew in importance when, in 1935, war games, in the form of military exercises including attack and defense, were held with more than 35,000 soldiers participating. This included aviators and military aircraft, as seen in this image. Later artwork recalling the event featured "enemy" planes spot lit in the skies above the camp. The success of the maneuvers and the advent of World War II caused Pine Camp to expand, eventually becoming the base it is today, which is home to the 10th Mountain Division and its Combat Aviation Brigade, which includes helicopters that may be seen in maneuvers over the Adirondacks. (Courtesy of Lynn Thornton.)

There may be no better way to view the impact of industry on the earth than by air. Located northeast of Newcomb, the Tahawus Mine first opened in the 1820s to extract iron ore and operated for a few decades. The 1940s saw the mine reopen to extract titanium; it was sometime between then and the 1970s that this image of the extensive open pits was taken. (Courtesy of SLFLARR.)

With the Saranac Lake area famous for its period as a tuberculosis care center, perhaps the most famous of those involved was Dr. Edward Trudeau, who established his practice and sanatorium there. Others, such as Elizabeth Wilmot Newcomb, were less well-known yet played an important role in the cure industry. This aerial photograph shows the idyllic setting of Stony Wold, the sanatorium founded by Newcomb on Lake Kushaqua in 1901. (Courtesy of SLFLARR.)

As Saranac Lake developed into a major center for tuberculosis research and treatment in the late 19th and early 20th centuries, more cure cottages, sanatoria, and hospitals were built, developed, and grew. In 1904, the New York State Hospital for Incipient Tuberculosis opened in Ray Brook, a hamlet between Lake Placid and Saranac Lake. From its inception, the hospital provided quality care in an environment that was meant to be congenial and comfortable, rather like a hotel. Patients who were well enough participated in outdoor activities, including sledding in winter and golf in summer, and indoor entertainment, such as live music and dances. It was also one of the few places where patients of color were admitted, including African American and indigenous patients. Patients sent postcards home to families featuring the hospital but few captured the scene as well as this c. 1950 aerial photograph, which shows the expansive nature of the hospital. (Courtesy of SLFLARR.)

In 1938, the US Post Office Department was making an effort to promote airmail: a quicker way to get letters and important correspondence to their destination. Although airmail in the United States began in 1911 and as a scheduled service in 1918, it was slower to be used in more rural settings. To promote the service and to commemorate the 20th anniversary of the first scheduled service, the US Post Office Department created National Air Mail Week May 15–21, 1938. This week saw more than one exciting flight, including the first airmail flight from the Adirondacks, which took place on May 19. Departing from Marcy Field, Keene physician and keen aviator Alphonso Goff made the flight in an Aeronca C-3. One year earlier, production on the C-3 model had stopped because it did not meet newer regulations for airworthiness, yet Dr. Goff's flight was successful, as were his many others. This envelope was one of those flown in celebration of the first airmail flight out of the Adirondacks. (Courtesy of KVL.)

Five

COMMERCIAL FLIGHT
AND AIRPORT LIFE

Although aviation increasingly became part of life in the Adirondacks, it often took a few years for proper airfields and airports to come to fruition. In June 1946, the first commercial flight out of the airport at Lake Clear departed, with the first hangar built a year later. The Esso-branded windsock, a bright orange and blue, would have been a useful weather tool. (Courtesy of SLFLARR.)

The creation of the airport at Lake Clear not only created opportunities for commercial flight, but it also enabled wealthy individuals with private planes the chance to arrive at their Adirondack camps in luxury. Marjorie Merriweather Post, a businesswoman and Post cereal heiress, was one such traveler. Her private plane, a Vickers Viscount named *Merriweather*, transported Post, her family, and guests to Topridge, her expansive Great Camp on Upper St. Regis Lake. At one point, the camp consisted of more than 65 buildings and housed Post's collections of art and Native American artifacts. The *Merriweather* was no ordinary private plane but rather a British-built passenger jet befitting an heiress, with luxurious seating for 22 (instead of the standard 44), couches, and large, oval windows. The *Merriweather* made regular trips to Saranac Lake as well as Florida, Connecticut, and beyond. (Courtesy of SLFLARR.)

Taken for granted now, air travel was once a novelty and a source of great excitement for the traveler. The identities of these smiling gentlemen at the Saranac Lake Regional Airport—now Adirondack Regional Airport—are not presently known, but their enthusiasm and a few small details make it easy to imagine adventure is not far. From the moment George Gray arrived in a Wright Model B biplane in 1912, many Saranac Lake area residents were hooked on aviation. The airport at Lake Clear offered ample opportunities for private pilots to offer sightseeing tours, travel with their families, and connect to other cities and towns. In the 1940s, several locals started up a flying club, purchasing an Aeronca for the club's use. The plane in this image features an open cockpit; the gentleman second from the right is holding flying goggles in his hand, ideal for the uncertain weather up top. (Courtesy of SLFLARR.)

This image, along with several others in this book, comes from the collections of the Adirondack Experience: The Museum on Blue Mountain Lake, which was founded in 1957 as the Adirondack Museum by Harold Hochschild. Hochschild, a wealthy businessman and philanthropist, grew up visiting Blue Mountain Lake as a boy, where his family had a share in the expansive property known as Eagle Nest. Hochschild's father and the other owners were prominent businessmen. At some point in the camp's history, an airfield was installed, making trips to and from the camp easier for all. Although railroads were more plentiful and well-traveled in the Adirondacks at the time, they could not compete with the ease of one's own aircraft. By the time this image was taken in the early 1970s, Adirondack passenger railroads were a thing of the past. (Courtesy of ADKX.)

Visiting relatives several hundred miles away is an easy week-end round-trip flight for this Stinson Voyager owner and family.

America's *most useful* personal plane!
The great new *Stinson* Voyager for '47!

Some owners of the stunning new *21st Anniversary* Stinson Voyager tell us they bought it because it is so easy to fly.

Others chose it because of its dependability, its inherent Stinson stability, and its ability to get in and out of small fields.

But *all* Voyager owners agree that perhaps the feature that pleases them most is the supreme *utility* of this popular "fly-anywhere" plane.

The Voyager carries a useful load of 965 lbs. Cruises at 125 m.p.h. Maximum speed, 134 m.p.h. Take-off run, only 590 ft. Rate of climb, 755 f.p.m. Service ceiling, 15,650 ft. Stops in 290 ft. after landing.

Flaps for quick take-offs and slow, short landings . . . built-in wing slots for safety. Inherently spin-resistant. Oleo spring-draulic landing gear for smooth, cushioned landings.

Two-way radio, with dome loudspeaker . . . landing and navigation lights . . . starter . . . dual engine mufflers . . . hydraulic brakes. Cabin interiors, designed by Henry Dreyfuss, are sound-proofed and air-conditioned.

See the beautiful new 4-place Voyager at your Stinson dealer's, or write for free illustrated brochure to Stinson Division, Consolidated Vultee Aircraft Corporation, Dept. C, Wayne, Mich.

Stinson

FOR 21 YEARS—AMERICA'S
MOST USEFUL PERSONAL PLANES

See The Stinson Flying Station Wagon — America's first personal "cargo" plane. Specially reinforced cargo compartment (94 cu. ft.) in 2-tone plywood paneling with tie-down straps. A side-loading baggage compartment offers an additional 11 cubic feet of carrying space. Load capacity: pilot, full gas tanks (40 gallons) and 552 cargo pounds. The two rear seats can be replaced to make it a 4-place plane.

It may be hard to believe now, but there was a time when small airplanes were advertised as an ideal means of transportation for families, just as minivans and SUVs are today. In this 1947 advertisement from the Stinson Aircraft Company, the Stinson 150 is billed as "America's most useful personal plane!" offering comfortable, safe flights for business as well as family trips. The Stinson was popular across the country as well as in the Adirondacks. Santa's Workshop founder Julian Reiss flew his family in a Stinson 150, which was also used to deliver gifts from Santa to underprivileged children. Other Stinson aircraft flew throughout the Adirondacks, including a Stinson Detroiter that was docked at and operated from the Eagle Bay Hotel on Fourth Lake. The Detroiter was an older and larger aircraft than the 150.

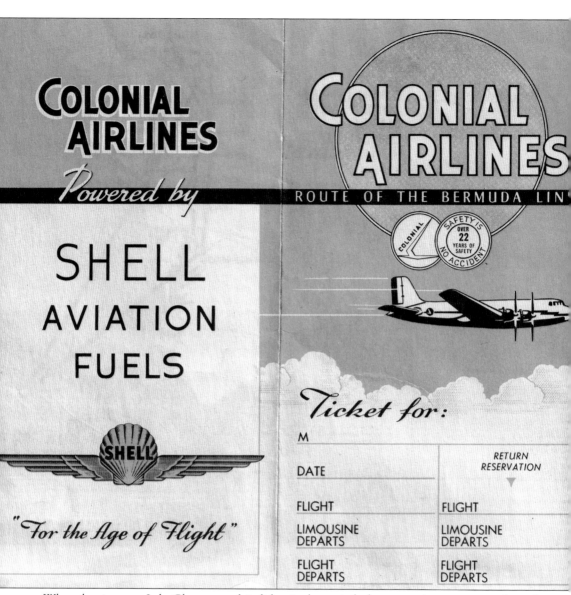

When the airport at Lake Clear opened, it did so in the period when extensive passenger rail travel in the Adirondacks was on the decline and before the arrival of the interstate highway system. Thus, travel to or from many locations in the Adirondacks could be a protracted experience. Passenger service at the airport began in 1946, with Colonial Airlines offering daily flights to LaGuardia Airport in New York City and points beyond. Once common, this ticket folder, which doubled as a handy brochure, would have held a traveler's paper ticket, which would have been purchased at a Colonial Airlines office. The illustration on the cover shows a Douglas DC-4, the aircraft Colonial used on its longer haul flights and differentiated here from the DC-3, which Colonial also flew, by the number of engines. (Courtesy of Historic Saranac Lake Collection [2009.9.1].)

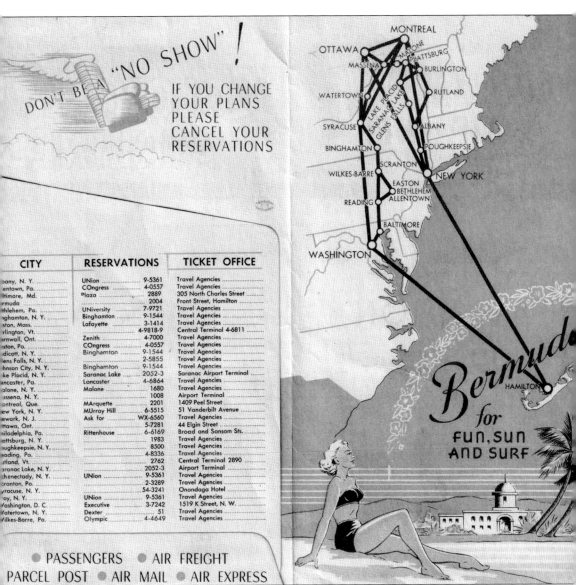

DON'T BE A "NO SHOW"!

IF YOU CHANGE YOUR PLANS PLEASE CANCEL YOUR RESERVATIONS

CITY	RESERVATIONS		TICKET OFFICE
...bany, N. Y.	UNion	9-5361	Travel Agencies
...entown, Pa.	COngress	4-0557	Travel Agencies
...ltimore, Md.	Plaza	2889	305 North Charles Street
...rmuda		2004	Front Street, Hamilton
...thlehem, Pa.	UNiversity	7-9721	Travel Agencies
...nghamton, N. Y.	Binghamton	9-1544	Travel Agencies
...ston, Mass.	Lafayette	3-1414	Travel Agencies
...rlington, Vt.		4-9818-9	Central Terminal 4-6811
...rnwall, Ont.	Zenith	4-7000	Travel Agencies
...ston, Pa.	COngress	4-0557	Travel Agencies
...dicott, N. Y.	Binghamton	9-1544	Travel Agencies
...ens Falls, N. Y.		2-5855	Travel Agencies
...hnson City, N. Y.	Binghamton	9-1544	Travel Agencies
...ke Placid, N. Y.	Saranac Lake	2052-3	Saranac Airport Terminal
...ncaster, Pa.	Lancaster	4-6864	Travel Agencies
...alone, N. Y.	Malone	1680	Travel Agencies
...assena, N. Y.		1008	Airport Terminal
...ontreal, Que.	MArquette	2201	1409 Peel Street
...ew York, N. Y.	MUrray Hill	6-5515	51 Vanderbilt Avenue
...ewark, N. J.	Ask for	WX-6560	Travel Agencies
...ttawa, Ont.		5-7281	44 Elgin Street
...iladelphia, Pa.	Rittenhouse	6-6169	Broad and Sansom Sts.
...attsburg, N. Y.		1983	Travel Agencies
...oughkeepsie, N. Y.		8500	Travel Agencies
...ading, Pa.		4-8336	Central Terminal 2890
...utland, Vt.		2762	Travel Agencies
...aranac Lake, N. Y.		2052-3	Airport Terminal
...chenectady, N. Y.	UNion	9-5361	Travel Agencies
...cranton, Pa.		2-3289	Travel Agencies
...yracuse, N. Y.		54-3241	Onondaga Hotel
...oy, N. Y.	UNion	9-5361	Travel Agencies
...Vashington, D. C.	Executive	3-7242	1519 K Street, N. W.
...Vatertown, N. Y.	Dexter	51	Travel Agencies
...Vilkes-Barre, Pa.	Olympic	4-4649	Travel Agencies

● PASSENGERS ● AIR FREIGHT
PARCEL POST ● AIR MAIL ● AIR EXPRESS

For a traveler departing Saranac Lake on a Colonial Airlines passenger jet, the East Coast was opened up for air travel without requiring a lengthy drive to Montréal or Albany. As shown in the interior of the Colonial Airlines brochure/ticket folder, the primary destination for Colonial passengers was Bermuda, where "fun, sun, and surf" awaited. And while Colonial's easy flight (only 90 minutes) from the Adirondacks to New York made many more connections possible, newspaper reports from the 1950s show that, at times, Colonial wished to discontinue winter service or transfer service to Plattsburgh and was not considered overly reliable. Colonial Airlines merged with Eastern Airlines in 1956, and eventually, the regular scheduled service to Saranac Lake ended. (Courtesy of Historic Saranac Lake Collection [2009.9.1].)

Two couples arriving by Colonial Airlines Ski-Plane for happy days of winter sports.

Some of the earliest flights into the Adirondacks were on skis in place of wheels or pontoons, but the introduction of Colonial Airlines' passenger service to Saranac Lake brought new meaning to the term "ski-plane." Although this liner landed on wheels, the term was used to tempt customers to fly north to ski in the Adirondacks and Canada.

The total price on this carbon from a Colonial Airlines ticket receipt, dated February 24, 1954, shows that the cost of a single ticket from Saranac Lake to New York was $21.74, an amount that seems too good to be true today—because it is. When adjusted for inflation, that ticket would cost just over $248 today. (Courtesy of Historic Saranac Lake Collection [2009.9.1].)

Six

Tragic Endings and Close Calls

Sadly, crashes and near misses were also part of life for aviators, and pilots in the Adirondacks were no exception. In 1944, this Royal Canadian Air Force (RCAF) fighter, which was on a training flight, had to make an unexpected landing in Lake Pleasant, on a farmer's field. Fortunately, no one was injured in the event, and the RCAF retrieved the plane by truck a week later. (Courtesy of SLPHS Inc.)

On the evening of September 20, 1944, a Curtiss C-46 Commando belonging to the US Army Air Forces took off from the Syracuse Army Air Base. The flight was a nighttime navigational training mission that had a tragic ending. At some point in the flight, the aircraft crashed into the slope of Blue Ridge Mountain near Speculator and Benson at an elevation of 3,200 feet. Search and rescue efforts went on for several days with no sign of the plane or its crew members. It was not until the following August that the crash site was located by hikers searching for a different downed craft and reported the location of the C-46. Sadly, this would not be the last plane to go missing for an extended period of time in the wilds of the Adirondack Mountains. (Courtesy of ADKX.)

This image shows a Curtiss C-46, the same type of aircraft that crashed on September 20, 1944, in the air. This version of the C-46 was designed to hold 40 troops, but fortunately, because this mission was intended for navigational training, only three crew members were on board the ill-fated mission. After the crash site was discovered nearly one year later, the remains of the crew members were returned to their families. Today, pieces of the plane remain isolated in the forest, although a group of aviation crash historians later placed a plaque and a flag on the wreckage of one wing in honor of the crew's loss. This incident was one of the first known crashes of the C-46, which had entered military service only a few years before. It would, however, see successful action throughout World War II as a transport.

The Windhausen brothers' WACO biplane, seen here after a nose-down event in Beaver Lake, possibly in 1946 or 1947, had an interesting history before it even belonged to the aviator brothers. In 1939, the plane, then the property of the Reading Battery Company, crashed. The WACO was eventually purchased and registered in the name of Bud Windhausen, possibly replacing an American Eagle A-1, a plane designed as a training aircraft. Although the incident here looks bad, there were evidently no major injuries to the crew or the plane. Both Windhausen brothers were accomplished pilots, with Bud having been the chief test pilot for the Army Air Corps' Army Transport Command. In addition to the WACO and a Cessna, Bud Windhausen was also the owner of a Grumman amphibious boat, known as a Widgeon, of which at least one photograph of the craft on Adirondack waters still survives. (Courtesy of TOWHA.)

What appears to be a grim scene may not, in fact, have been fatal. Unfortunately, there have been enough plane crashes throughout the Adirondacks that not all are immediately identifiable. Kept in the collection of the Adirondack Research Room in Saranac Lake, this image, which features several canoes of people around the downed plane, may show a crash that occurred in 1939 in Polliwog Pond, a scenic location in the Saranac Lakes Wild Forest, near Saranac Inn. Newspaper reports from around the Adirondacks in the 1930s and 1940s detail a number of crashes, both fatal and nonfatal, and even one incident in which berry pickers saw a low-flying plane disappear, prompting a search by the state police, which found the plane upright after a smooth landing. In the incident at Polliwog Pond, one woman was injured while the other two occupants of the plane were unharmed. (Courtesy of SLFLARR.)

Despite the skills and tremendous efforts of aviators, weather and the environment occasionally got the best of even the finest pilots. Here, a tractor is used to pull a plane from a patch of thin ice it had broken through, despite landing on skis, which are just visible in the photograph. The incident was said to have taken place on Piseco Lake near the hangar owned by bush pilot John Knox, who had a seaplane base and was, interestingly enough, a member of the Knox Gelatine family. (Courtesy of HCH.)

A startling crash took place in Wilmington in 1928 when a WACO biplane collided with the steeple of a Nazarene church. The plane was piloted by George Walker, president of the Albany Air Service, which offered brief sightseeing flights at the nearby airport. Two local boys were in the plane with Walker, but they were completely unharmed in the incident. Despite the mangled wreckage of the plane, Walker sustained only two broken bones, both of which were located in his feet. He remained in the hospital in nearby Lake Placid for several days to recover from the alarming nature of the crash. A section of the roof of the church was torn off, and despite the accident occurring on a Sunday, no one inside the church was injured either. (Courtesy of Town Historian Collection, WHS.)

Many early aviators were those who could afford the indulgence of buying a plane without worrying about making a living through barnstorming and air races. One such aviator was Robert J. Collier, heir to the *Collier's Magazine* fortune and publishing company. As a young man, Collier was intensely interested in aviation, eventually becoming a friend of Wilbur Wright, purchasing his own Wright Model B, and taking on the role of president of the Aero Club of America. Through the Aero Club, Collier was involved in the staging of massive air shows and competitions and commissioned the Collier Trophy, an award still given today for aviation and aeronautic excellence. Collier owned a massive Great Camp on Bluff Point on Raquette Lake, which still stands today. Around the lake, Collier was well-known for his use of a large, impressively fast boat.

In the summer of 1912, Collier had wood pontoons added to his Wright Model B in place of wheels and had the entire plane shipped to Raquette Lake via railroad in a series of freight cars, causing no end of excitement in the town. Collier's intention was to fly the plane from his dock at Bluff Point, and had he been successful, it would have made him the first man to fly over the Adirondacks, being a few months ahead of George Gray's October flight to Saranac Lake. Unfortunately, upon takeoff, the Wright Model B (similar to the Model B pictured here) crashed into the lake for unknown reasons. Incredibly, no one was injured in the incident, and although the plane was recovered from the waters of Raquette Lake, another attempt was not made. The plane left the area as it arrived, via railway freight cars. Collier is said to have also crashed his boat at the lake. Collier died a short six years later, at the age of 42, while at Raquette Lake. (Courtesy of WSU.)

Now...that there are others

AERONCA'S LEADERSHIP IS PROVEN

From 1928 to 1951, the Aeronautical Corporation of America, shortened to Aeronca, manufactured popular light aircraft for use by the general aviation community, including planes such as that seen in this advertisement. In December 1941, a two-passenger Aeronca belonging to a brother and sister from Ticonderoga was stolen by two 23-year-old men, who took off in the plane at Port Henry and subsequently crashed it into a pasture located between Moriah and Port Henry around 5:00 a.m. After breaking into the hangar, the plane was pushed out to the runway with one of the young men, who had no pilot's license and had never soloed, at the controls. The young man died in the crash, while his friend was badly injured.

Whiteface Mountain, now known for its status as a popular ski resort and the site of the Alpine events in the 1980 Olympic Winter Games, also has a sad aviation history. In February 1943, the two crew members of a Royal Canadian Air Force (RCAF) training flight were killed in a nighttime crash on the east side of the mountain. The Lockheed Hudson, a reconnaissance and light bomber aircraft, crashed in a blinding snowstorm, which was attributed as the cause of the crash. Rescue efforts to reach the crash commenced almost immediately, the plane having been heard flying low over Wilmington, but the depth of the snow, which reached five to six feet, slowed progress. Because of the snowstorm, the crew was attempting to follow state roads to return to their base located over the border in Lachine. Perhaps most tragically, the pilots had landing lights on and appeared to be looking for a place to land but found none before the crash. Pictured here is another RCAF Lockheed Hudson.

The wintry crash in this undated photograph may be evidence of an incident that occurred on Saranac Lake's Lake Flower on December 29, 1929. Many winter flights took place between Saranac Lake and Lake Placid, with hotel owners having hired pilots and their planes—equipped with skis instead of wheels or floats—to offer sightseeing tours between the two villages. The December 29 accident occurred when a plane from Lake Placid attempted to return after a trip to Saranac Lake. The pilot set the plane down safely on Lake Flower, but the thinness of the ice caused the plane to break through while taking off. Undoubtedly a frightening incident, no one was injured, although a local newspaper reported the passengers were uncomfortably drenched. Theirs was not the only incident around New Year 1930: two teenagers from Malone damaged their plane in a similar snowstorm near Newcomb just one day later. (Courtesy of SLFLARR.)

Seven

UNIQUE VENTURES AND CURIOUS OUTINGS

Beyond adventure and service, pioneering flights, and tragedy, Adirondack skies have also hosted aviation antics, daredevil stunts, and other flying curiosities. In 1929, Mary, Lady Heath, dazzled crowds in Lake Placid in 1929 as part of a traveling air show. The first British woman to obtain a pilot's license, she was one of the most famous women in the world by the mid-1920s, known for long-distance flights and air races.

FRANKLIN COUNTY

MALONE, N. Y.

September 14, 15, 16, 17, '26

Great Agricultural and Industrial Exhibition

WONDERFUL ATTRACTIONS

ROBINSON'S ELEPHANTS In New and Unusual Acts

GATES' FLYING CIRCUS

Doing Most Daring Stunts in Aeroplanes

MAUD GILL TRIO Remarkable Acrobats

During the 1920s, flying circuses and air carnivals were an incredibly popular attraction around the country, moving from town to town just like any other circus. A variety of dangerous, exhilarating stunt flying was performed, along with appearances by world-famous aviators. Such flying circuses drew large crowds of spectators, and many of the circuses also offered non-pilots the chance to experience brief, relatively affordable flights. In 1926, the Gates Flying Circus, created by aviator Ivan Gates, toured New York state with the distinction of being the most successful flying circus in the nation at that time. The circus, with its Standard J two-seater aircraft modified to fit passengers, visited Lake Placid and was prominently advertised for its presence at the annual Franklin County Fair in Malone. Posters for the Gates Flying Circus promised acrobatics and the "greatest aggregation of dare devil performers ever assembled."

One of the aviators in the Gates Flying Circus was Clyde Pangborn, who was famous for, among other stunts, attempting to transfer from a moving car to an airplane via a rope ladder. In this attempt on the beach in San Diego, Pangborn missed the ladder and tumbled across the sand. Pangborn's nickname was "Upside-Down," thanks to his death-defying stunts, which included changing from one plane to another mid-air. Following the end of the Gates Flying Circus, Pangborn dedicated himself to setting long-distance flight records. Because the Gates Flying Circus offered so many free or inexpensive flights to ordinary passengers (numbering in the thousands), a number of barnstormers of the next generation had their first flights with Pangborn. By the time of his natural death in 1958, Pangborn had logged more than 24,000 hours as a pilot.

Over the Fourth of July weekend in 1930, Lake Placid was the site of another spectacular flying circus. Held over three days, the event included formation stunt flying, demonstrations of the latest aircraft, a steeplechase to Whiteface Mountain and back, and wingwalking by Billy Bomar, pictured here with fellow wingwalker Ova Kinney in the type of demonstration performed in Lake Placid.

Also in the flying circus, German aviatrix Antonie Strassmann was among those with top billing. A bit of a daredevil, Strassmann believed in pilots being able to handle any aircraft in any weather. Her US tours, which included exhibits of model aircraft, helped her promote aviation and introduced her to scores of young women with an interest in flying, who would crowd around her aircraft.

While snowmobiles have been common throughout the Adirondacks for several decades, surely some of the most unique were to be found in the Inlet and Old Forge area. At one point, a man by the name of Elton LeFevre was the owner of a snowmobile crafted from airplane parts. With an enclosed "cockpit," door, rooftop light, and long runners, the snowmobile—or "air sled," as it was known—was a two-person creation of the Polaris company. A few years earlier, before his move to Inlet, pilot Harold Scott created a homegrown snowmobile from a variety of recycled parts, including a Harley-Davidson motorcycle engine and the propeller of an airplane. (Courtesy of TOWHA.)

The Goodyear company, which built its first airship in 1925, had a tradition of naming its airships after America's Cup yachts. NC-7A, which visited Saranac Lake and is seen here, was named *Puritan*. Built in 1928, the *Puritan I* made its first flight in July 1928 and was regularly upgraded in the years following, until a September 1938 hurricane in Massachusetts wrecked the airship. The *Puritan* was not the only airship to be seen in the Adirondacks—the *Los Angeles*, then the largest dirigible in the world, made several flights over the Adirondacks in 1928 and 1930—but it may have been the only one to land. (Courtesy of SLFLARR.)

From 1897 until the present, with a few years off on occasion—such as during wartime—Saranac Lake has celebrated the coldest season with its annual Winter Carnival, an event that began as a one-day festival and now lasts for more than a week. Carnival began as a project of the Pontiac Club, a local organization that counted community leaders among its members and which sought to encourage winter sports. Winter sports were also encouraged—even as a spectator sport—for tuberculosis patients, the cold air having been said to be good for the lungs. The carnival parade and its decorated floats have long been part of the carnival, beginning in 1898. In 1907, one group entered a mock dirigible, pulled by flag-draped horses. Dirigibles were in the news throughout the early 20th century, particularly as they began to be used by military forces; the cold temperatures in Saranac Lake and a 1907 attempt to fly an airship to the North Pole may have helped inspire this float. (Courtesy of SLFLARR.)

THE GOODYEAR "PURITAN"
A Small American Non-Rigid Airship

THREE years ago the Goodyear Tyre and Rubber Co., of Akron, Ohio, constructed an interesting little sporting airship, called the "Pilgrim" (see FLIGHT for May 6, 1926). Just recently, the Goodyear Zeppelin Corp. which is a subsidiary of the Goodyear Tyre and Rubber Co., launched their first airship, the "Puritan," a new and improved version of the "Pilgrim." We are able this week to give some brief particulars and an illustration of this new airship.

The "Puritan" is a marked advance on the "Pilgrim" in that it is somewhat larger and has a wider cruising range, higher speeds and greater lifting capacity. Powered with two radial air cooled-engines, the "Puritan" has a cruising

110 ft. long, 30 ft. diameter, and of 53,000 cub. ft. capacity—are a strong keel within the envelope attaching the car to the envelope, a second rudder on the top fin for additional manœuvrability, and dual controls. A single swivelling "landing" wheel is also mounted below the car. The engines are equipped with automatic starters, and are geared to revolve the propellers in opposite directions, thus reducing the torque in the car, besides increasing the ship's stability and manœuvring capacities. Incidentally, it may be added, the ship can fly on one engine.

Dr. Karl Arnstein, formerly chief engineer of the German Zeppelin Co., and now associated with the Goodyear-Zeppelin

THE GOODYEAR "PURITAN": This small non-rigid airship was recently launched by the Goodyear-Zeppelin Corp. of Akron, Ohio. It is 128 ft. long and is fitted with two air-cooled radial engines. Inset is a view of the car, seated in which is P. W. Litchfield, President of the Goodyear companies.

Known today as blimps, the Goodyear company's dirigibles were originally known as airships, the term "blimp" having a somewhat mysterious origin, perhaps during World War II. The first Goodyear airships were made for the US Navy, but their successful flights and distinctive appearance in the skies led Goodyear to use them for advertising as well, a tradition that has continued into the 21st century. Impressively, the Puritan had a flying range of 550 miles, although the cab had room for only one pilot and two passengers.

In 1929, Adirondack skies saw the appearance of an unusual sight: massive piloted balloons. The balloons were competitors in a race originating in Pittsburgh, Pennsylvania. One, the *Goodyear VII*, landed successfully in Harkness, while another landed in the High Peaks north of Newcomb, with the unfortunate pilots lost in the woods for two days. Such was their distress that the pilots of the balloon had no idea what state they were in, and at one point, they climbed a nearby mountain to get a view of the surrounding countryside. After two cold days without food and water, the pilots happened upon a road and a crew of workers, who were astonished at the bedraggled appearance of the men. The top three finishers of the race they had been competing in qualified to compete in the Gordon Bennett Cup, the oldest balloon race in the world, seen here in 1912. The winner of the cup was the pilot of the *Goodyear VII*.

SANTA'S

Operation Toy Lift

Ten Tons of Toys to Poor and Orphaned Children
1953
The Fifth Year

Your Visit To Santa's Workshop
Aids and Supports This Work

FOR EIGHT DAYS STARTING DECEMBER FIRST, 1953 A HUGE PLANE LOANED BY ESSO STANDARD OIL FLEW SANTA, HIS GNOMES AND LOADS OF CAREFULLY SELECTED TOYS FROM NORTH POLE, N. Y. TO UNDERPRIVILEGED CHILDREN IN THIRTEEN STATES, TWO PROVINCES OF CANADA AND WASHINGTON, D. C.

Santa From North Pole, N.Y. Lands at Fall River, Mass.

Located in North Pole, New York, itself a part of the town of Wilmington, Santa's Workshop opened in July 1949, the brainchild of local businessman and philanthropist Julian Reiss, who, throughout his career, was involved in supporting charities and giving back to the underserved. Designed by local artist Arto Monaco and still in business today, Santa's Workshop has long brought the magic of Christmas to the summer months through a whimsical village where Santa and his reindeer are in residence. In 1949, Reiss began Operation Toylift, an effort to give gifts to underprivileged children throughout New York and Vermont.

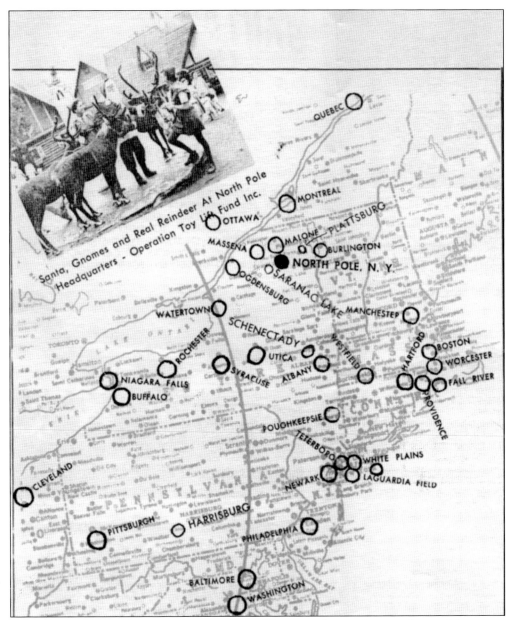

Santa, Gnomes and Real Reindeer At North Pole
Headquarters - Operation Toy Lift Fund Inc.

QUEBEC

MONTREAL

OTTAWA

PLATTSBURG

MASSENA MALONE BURLINGTON

NORTH POLE, N.Y.

OGDENSBURG

SARANAC LAKE MANCHESTER

WATERTOWN

SCHENECTADY

ROCHESTER UTICA WESTFIELD HARTFORD BOSTON

SYRACUSE ALBANY WORCESTER

NIAGARA FALLS FALL RIVER

BUFFALO PROVIDENCE

POUGHKEEPSIE

TETERBORO WHITE PLAINS

CLEVELAND NEWARK LAGUARDIA FIELD

PITTSBURGH HARRISBURG

PHILADELPHIA

BALTIMORE WASHINGTON

Reiss, an accomplished private pilot, initially used his own plane, a four-seat Stinson Voyager, to deliver gifts, particularly to small communities. The sight of Santa himself at the controls was a delight to many. Operation Toylift was a considerable success, with gifts donated by local businesses and purchased via the donations of the wishing well at Santa's Workshop. As the success grew, the need for a larger aircraft grew as well. Six years after Operation Toylift began, Esso Standard Oil loaned the use of a much larger plane, a Curtiss C-46, nicknamed "the Silver Sleigh." With the use of the C-46, Operation Toylift, along with Santa and a team of "gnomes," was able to expand, eventually delivering gifts to children in 13 US states, the District of Columbia, and two Canadian provinces.

Santa and his team were always greeted by joyful children of all ages. At each stop on an ambitious schedule, children from orphanages, hospitals, schools for the deaf, and children's homes were brought to local airports to experience the arrival of the Silver Sleigh and receive gifts. Each year, roughly 10 tons of gifts were distributed to children in need by Santa and the Silver Sleigh. The flights ceased in the mid-1960s, but Santa's Workshop has continued to raise funds and donate gifts to underprivileged children to this day. (Both, courtesy of Santa's Workshop Inc. Collection, WHS.)

Santa Claus has always found novel ways to travel through the Adirondacks, whether by sleigh, airplane, or even helicopter. In this unusual image, Santa does not appear to be delivering the typical gifts of the season but rather bundles of newspapers on a Tupper Lake rooftop, in a new role as a paperboy. Visible behind the helicopter are the tall smokestack and water tower of the Oval Wood Dish Company, a Tupper Lake landmark. Although the Oval Wood Dish Company had its own runway starting around 1950, Santa appears to have landed on a rooftop in the vicinity of Park Street, one of the village's business districts. (Courtesy of GNML.)

Christmas Greetings
The humming of his airship on the frosty air
Tells us that Santa is winging from his lair.

As airplanes were increasingly seen in Adirondack skies and in the newspapers, Santa Claus got in on the action as well. In each of these postcards, Santa appears minus his traditional reindeer in biplanes laden with wrapped gifts, a sack full of toys, and holiday greenery. Both models are very early pusher planes featuring a double elevator at the front of the aircraft. The earliest aircraft, including the Wright Flyer successfully flown in 1903 by Wilbur and Orville Wright, had elevators in the front to control pitch and generate lift; this style would be copied by other aircraft manufacturers in the United States and abroad. Both of these postcards were sent in the 1910s. General stores and shops throughout Adirondack towns, such as Kollecker's in Saranac Lake, likely carried postcards such as these.

The earliest planes were not intended for comfort, as this image clearly shows. This Wright biplane has two seats, although many other planes of the era had only one. This is most likely a Wright Model B, the same model aircraft flown by George Gray. (Courtesy of Library of Congress.)

Born in Au Sable Forks in 1913, Arto Monaco became one of the most beloved figures in the Adirondacks. With his natural artistic talent encouraged by neighbor Rockwell Kent, Monaco spent decades creating charming, whimsical toys, illustrations, and theme parks, including Santa's Workshop and the now-gone Land of Make Believe. In this image for a coloring book, Monaco captured the spirit and adventure of Adirondack flying. (Courtesy of ADKX.)

DISCOVER THOUSANDS OF LOCAL HISTORY BOOKS FEATURING MILLIONS OF VINTAGE IMAGES

Arcadia Publishing, the leading local history publisher in the United States, is committed to making history accessible and meaningful through publishing books that celebrate and preserve the heritage of America's people and places.

Find more books like this at
www.arcadiapublishing.com

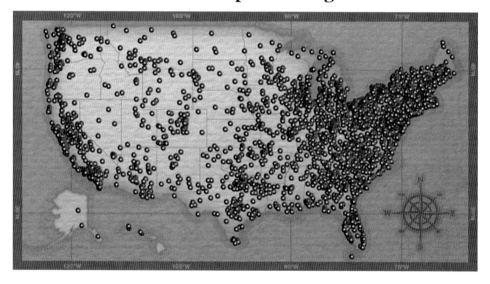

Search for your hometown history, your old stomping grounds, and even your favorite sports team.

Consistent with our mission to preserve history on a local level, this book was printed in South Carolina on American-made paper and manufactured entirely in the United States. Products carrying the accredited Forest Stewardship Council (FSC) label are printed on 100 percent FSC-certified paper.

MADE IN THE  USA